Advance Praise for *Built To Sell*

"FANTASTIC! Small businesses *need* this book. So many business owners have the dream of building a business that's bigger than themselves, and getting away from the tyranny of constantly putting out fires. John's book is an entertaining, to-the-point way of showing them how to do it. They might just find they like their business much better and not even want to sell later. But if they do sell, they'll get much more value from following the book's advice."
   - Anita Campbell
     Editor-In-Chief, Small Business Trends

"As we've always advised at StartupNation, the end depends upon the beginning. *Built To Sell*, like other great business books, brings into clarity the game-changing importance of clearly envisioning the destiny of your business. But even more, it tells you how to bring that destiny to life."
   - Rich Sloan
     Co-founder and chief startupologist of StartupNation

"*Built to Sell* reminds me of Eliyahu M. Goldratt's *The Goal*, in the way that the valuable lessons about successfully exiting a service business are intertwined with Alex Stapleton's compelling story. Alex's story drew me in immediately. Any current or aspiring service business owner should read *Built to Sell* and take heed of John Warrillow's valuable lessons and Alex Stapleton's enriching and engaging experience."
   - Mike Handelsman
     General Manager, Bizbuysell.com

BUILT
TO
SELL

BUILT
TO
SELL

Turn Your Business into One You Can Sell

JOHN WARRILLOW

flipjetmedia

ISBN 978-0-9864803-1-7
Hardcover ISBN: 978-0-9864803-0-0

Publisher's Cataloging-in-Publication Data

Library and Archives Canada Cataloguing in Publication

Warrillow, John, 1971-
    Built to sell : turn your business into one you can sell/John Warrillow.
ISBN 978-0-9864803-1-7 (pbk.).–ISBN 978-0-9864803-0-0 (bound)
    1. Sale of business enterprises. I. Title.
HD1393.25.W37 2010   658.1'64   C2009-907021-9

First Edition

Flip Jet Media Inc.
27 Atlantic Ave.
Toronto, ON M6K 2E7
Canada

Printed in U.S.A.

TABLE OF CONTENTS

Foreword

In almost three decades at *Inc.* magazine—first as senior editor, then executive editor, then editor-at-large—I have had many great mentors, and they've given me an extraordinary education in entrepreneurship. Among the many things I've learned from them has been the fundamental paradox that lies at the heart of company-building, at least as it is practiced by the smartest entrepreneurs: You should always run a company as if it will last forever, and yet you should also strive constantly to maximize its value, building in the qualities that allow it to be sold at any moment for the highest price buyers are paying for businesses like yours.

That's the philosophy of Jack Stack, the co-founder and CEO of SRC Holdings Corp. in Springfield, Mo., with whom I have written two books, *The Great Game of Business* and *A Stake in the Outcome*, that explore the mechanisms he and his colleagues have used to create such an enterprise. It's also the philosophy of Norm Brodsky, the serial entrepreneur with whom I have written another book, *Street Smarts* (formerly *The Knack*), as well as a long-running column in *Inc.* of the same name.

And it's the philosophy of John Warrillow. John, in fact, refers to this approach as having an "options strategy," as opposed to an "exit strategy." The idea is to have as many choices in the future as possible. When you follow an options strategy, he says, you "build systems and a management team around you so that if a buyer comes along, or you decide it's the right time to get out, you have a sellable business. Or so that you can install a president and move into a chairman's role, which is a kind of quasi-exit. Or so that you can stay involved day-to-day and work on building an enduring company that can go on without you."

The point is that the best businesses are sellable, and smart businesspeople believe that you should build a company to be sold *even if you have no intention of cashing out or stepping back anytime soon.* If you share that belief, this book is right up your alley. John does a masterful job in *Built To Sell* of illuminating the qualities that business buyers look for in a company, and he does it in a thoroughly enjoyable and engaging manner: by telling a story. Although Alex Stapleton—the lead character in the story—owns an advertising agency, the fundamental lessons he learns apply to any business, and reading about them can only serve to sharpen your thinking about how to make your own company sellable, no matter what type of business you are in.

John is certainly the right person to turn to for advice on this subject. Few people know the world of small business better than he does. I first heard about him in connection with a conference that his business, Warrillow & Co., organized every year to help Fortune 500 marketers figure out how to sell to small companies. The conference had acquired a reputation as the premier event for learning what smaller businesses wanted and how best to reach them. In addition to the conferences, Warrillow & Co. produced in-depth research papers on small business, based on annual surveys of some 10,000 business owners. A hundred giant corporations paid the firm substantial fees for access to those papers, as well as for the insights John and his associates had developed along the way. John himself hosted a nationally syndicated radio show on entrepreneurship. That's actually how he came to start his business: Big companies began approaching him for advice on reaching the small business market. He went on to sell Warrillow & Co. in 2008, which he couldn't have done without building a company that could continue to thrive without him.

And that's why this book is so good. John Warrillow has studied entrepreneurs; he's interviewed hundreds of them on the radio; he's built his own company around the small business market; and he's sold that business to someone else. If you want to find out what it really takes to build a sellable business, it's always best to listen first to someone who has done it himself. John Warrillow is your man.

Bo Burlingham
Editor-at-large, Inc. magazine and author of
Small Giants: Companies That Choose to Be Great Instead of Big

Preface

This book is about how to create a sellable business. It's the story of an imaginary business owner named Alex Stapleton who wants to sell his service business but discovers that nobody wants to buy it because he *is* the business. Alex's problem is that he has the most experience in his field so he does most of the selling for his company. Not surprisingly, Alex's clients all want him to personally oversee their projects.

Stretched thin and running from one fire to the next, Alex reaches a plateau and finds it impossible to get to the next level with his business. When he decides to sell, Alex meets with his old friend and successful entrepreneur, Ted Gordon. The story unfolds as Ted teaches Alex how to turn his business into a sellable company.

While the story is fictional, Alex's experiences are very real for many business owners. There are approximately 23 million businesses in the United States and only a few hundred thousand are able to sell their company each year. That means for every small business owner who creates a business that someone will buy, there are about 100 businesses that do not sell. This book provides a framework and action plan for ensuring that you are the one in a hundred who has a sellable company.

This story is not an autobiography. Alex and Ted are an amalgam of the 15 years I have spent covering the small business market. My first exposure to the life of a business owner was as a floundering recent college grad when my parents took me to an awards show celebrating a group of successful entrepreneurs. I listened to their amazing life stories and decided to create a radio program to tell those stories. The radio feature was called "Today's Entrepreneur" and I interviewed a different entrepreneur every weekday for three years. I then spent 12 years building a research company designed to help enterprise companies target small businesses. We interviewed and surveyed more than 10,000 business owners each year in an effort to delve deep inside their heads. I've also woven in some of my own experiences, having started and exited four companies. I was lucky enough to have had a handful of mentors who collectively make up the sage wisdom embodied by the character of Ted Gordon.

There are many reasons for wanting to build a sellable business:

- your company may be your best shot at a comfortable retirement;
- you may want to start another business;
- you may need cash to deal with a divorce;
- you may want more time for yourself or financial freedom; or
- you may want to sleep better at night knowing that you *could* sell your business.

Whatever is motivating you to create a business that could be sold, I hope you find the story of Alex and Ted inspiring and helpful.

John Warrillow

1

A Company in Chaos

Alex Stapleton wheeled the Range Rover into the parking lot of First National Bank. He grabbed his portfolio from the back seat and sprinted to the doors. A quick check of his watch made it official: 9:06 a.m. He was late—again.

As a regular visitor, Alex's name was on the list at reception and the security guard waved him in. He found an open elevator and hit the button for the 18th floor. He took his first full breath of air since leaving his office.

John Stevens had worked at the bank for seven years. He'd landed a job as an account manager straight out of business school. He spent a few years lending money to small businesses and then got a job in marketing at the bank's head office. Premature bald, and pudgy, he seemed angry at life for the cards he'd been dealt. John had no formal training in marketing, yet he insisted on directing every detail of Alex's work.

"Sorry I'm late, John. Traffic was . . . "

"Did you bring the mock-ups?" John asked Alex impatiently.

Alex unzipped his portfolio, wiped his brow, and settled in for the long haul. He unveiled the first design and John didn't flinch. He waved Alex off the moment he began to explain the designer's vision for the piece.

"Let's see the next one."

After Alex presented all eight concepts, John took his time before selecting a design and then gave his instructions. He wanted the picture reduced, the font changed, and the red to be more orange red instead of the pink red selected by Alex's designer. John droned on with more feedback. Alex felt as if he were back in primary school. Despite being woefully unqualified, John seemed to relish his new role as art critic. Alex left the meeting room promising John another round of mock-ups by Monday morning. He pulled out of the parking lot feeling broken.

****

If John Stevens were the exception, Alex could have lived with it. Unfortunately, John represented the bulk of Alex's clients: marketing managers with crappy jobs who seemed to like pushing around their marketing agency.

Alex had started The Stapleton Agency eight years before, after a career at a blue-chip marketing agency. He started doing logos and brochures for small businesses and gradually moved up to becoming an Approved Vendor for First National Bank. Having Approved Vendor status meant that the bank paid their bills and kept The Stapleton Agency on a short list of alternative suppliers to their Agency of Record. When the bank's main marketing agency rejected smaller jobs, the bank summoned The Stapleton Agency.

When Alex started the agency, he dreamed of working on important campaigns with large budgets. He imagined directing models and actors between booze-soaked lunches with chief marketing officers. He wanted to be part of the scene. Instead, he was trying to figure out how to explain to his designer that she would need to work through the weekend because the client—a middle manager who had never taken a design course, doing a job he was completely unqualified for—wanted the red changed to "orange red."

****

The Stapleton Agency was located in a funky part of the city just west of downtown. Alex paid $4,000 a month for more space than he needed with the hope that it would impress clients. The office had all of the requisite touches befitting a creative shop: exposed brick walls, glass-encased boardroom, 12-foot-long boardroom table, and a permanently mounted overhead projector. Sadly, it rarely served its purpose—First National Bank insisted that Alex come to them.

He tried to slip into his office without his senior designer, Sarah Buckner, noticing but she heard his keys jangle. She looked up from her computer.

"How'd it go?"

"Pretty good. He had a few changes, but nothing major. I'll come see you in a few minutes."

With that, Alex went into his office and shut the door. He needed caffeine. The day's mail was on his desk and he quickly scanned it for the familiar blue and gold logo of First National Bank. He was expecting a check.

Alex collected his thoughts and prioritized the next few hours. He needed to get Sarah working on the First National Bank changes, go across town for lunch, get back to write a proposal, and find time to call his banker.

Sarah rolled her eyes as Alex delivered the news. He tried to present John's design instructions in such a way so as prevent squashing Sarah's motivation or further amplify the hatred she felt toward John Stevens and First National Bank. She accepted her sentence, donned her sound-canceling earphones to shut out the sorry world she found herself in, and set out to find the proper shade of orange red that would appease Lord Stevens.

Alex kicked himself for not standing up to John. He felt weak but the reality was The Stapleton Agency could not afford to lose First National Bank as a client. Last month, the bank amounted to $48,000 of The Stapleton Agency's $120,000 in total billings. Alex, Sarah, and the other seven employees of The Stapleton Agency needed First National Bank.

****

Traffic was heavy on the way across town and Alex was late for his second meeting of the day. Sandy Garmalo sat at the table sipping San Pellegrino. She ran the marketing department for a law firm, and had been Alex's client for five years. The law firm never generated huge billings for The Stapleton Agency but they were steady, which required Alex to spring for lunch once a quarter. For Sandy, Alex's lunches were a nice escape from the overbearing lawyers she served.

The waiter arrived and asked if they would like a drink. Alex was about to ask for a Diet Coke when Sandy pre-empted him.

"I'll have a glass of your house white."

Alex had too much to do that afternoon but knew that letting Sandy drink alone would make lunch awkward.

"I'll have the same," Alex said, promising himself that he would nurse one glass.

Sandy was a divorced 50-something woman, 10 years older than Alex. She enjoyed flirting with him and Alex obliged, knowing that a little harmless flirting would keep the projects flowing to The Stapleton Agency.

Appetizers were picked at. More wine arrived. Sandy rambled on about the lawyers she worked for. Alex became increasingly less interested in Sandy's prattle. Eventually, the waiter cleared the plates and dessert was offered and refused. Sandy requested a coffee. Resigning himself to another 10 minutes of meaningless banter, Alex ordered an espresso.

The bill came and Alex produced his credit card. One of the perks of owning The Stapleton Agency was the ability to charge $8,000 worth of expenses per month on his card, which generated a nice stash of travel points that he promised himself to use this year for a vacation with his family. Alex sat nervously as the waiter went away and asked the credit gods for a little bit of understanding. He'd been late paying off his balance last month and was cut off until his account was back in good standing. His bill was due again some time this week and he hoped the date had not passed.

The waiter returned. The card had snuck under the watchful eyes of the bank's credit department. Alex smiled, retrieved the card, signed the receipt, and got on with the business of extracting himself from lunch. Sandy made some vague overtures about upcoming projects she would need The Stapleton

Agency's help with. Alex feigned interest and eventually made his escape.

Alex stopped at Starbucks on the way home for a second coffee, which he hoped would sober him up enough to write the proposal he desperately needed to have accepted.

****

The Request for Proposal had come in from Urban Sports Warehouse, a local sporting goods retailer. They had grown tired of their agency and were looking for a new marketing firm to handle all of their work, which included newspaper ads, local radio spots, store banners, and an e-commerce-enabled website.

Alex knew that his team could handle the print ads and in-store signage. He had a friend at a production house who could help with the radio work. Most of the website work would be outsourced, but Urban Sports Warehouse did not need to know that.

After pasting the requisite drivel about the history of his agency, its creative credentials, and awards, Alex began to estimate his fees. There would be hard costs for studio time, proofs, and freelance web designers. Then he tried to estimate the staff's time. He billed his designers at $200 per hour and his own time at $300 per hour. These were largely arbitrary rates established over time by researching how much competitors charged.

Alex hated the process of estimating hours. He knew it was an inexact science and that his actual hours invested would have no resemblance to what he was estimating. Creating marketing material was such an iterative process that there was no way to estimate his time accurately.

After four hours of writing and doing some fuzzy math, the proposal was done. It was 6:30 p.m. and he had missed the FedEx guy for the day so he dropped the proposal off at the depot on the way home. He handed it to the clerk and hoped that Urban Sports Warehouse would be the client that would finally make him less reliant on First National Bank and the likes of John Stevens.

Given the late hour, it was probably safe to call Mary Pradham's office. Mary was his account manager at First National Bank, where he had been required to move his business banking in recognition of making it onto the bank's Approved Vendor list. Mary had kids so she usually left by 5:30 p.m. Alex was bumping up against his $150,000 line of credit. Ironically, he was expecting a check from Mary's employer today but it hadn't arrived.

Alex left Mary a voice mail, hoping that it would buy him a few days. The Stapleton Agency provided Alex with a decent income and a great vehicle for tax-write-offs. He ran the Range Rover through the business and was sure to keep the bill whenever he ate out with friends. He had been able to give himself a bonus of $150,000 last year on top of his $100,000 annual salary. Not bad, but the cash flow was lumpy and this wasn't his first late night call to Mary.

The Decision

Alex met a client for breakfast on Monday morning. It was after 10:00 a.m. when he got to his office. When he arrived, he knew it was going to be a bad day. Taped to his door was a note from

Sarah:

Sunday, 4:00 p.m.
Alex:
We need to talk.
Sarah

This was not going to be good. He'd hired his best designer away from a rival agency last year. Sarah was needed for all of the First National Bank work. He walked over to Sarah's desk. She looked up from her work.

"Let's do this in your office."

Alex turned and walked back to his office. Sarah followed and closed the door. She didn't waste any time.

"Look, Alex, I like you and the rest of the team here but I'm going back to my old job at Curve Designs. I'll wrap up the brochure project for First National, but when that's done, I'm out."

Alex felt rejected. He knew that there was nothing he could say or do. Working the weekend to revise the First National Bank brochure to accommodate a client who knew nothing about design had finally pushed Sarah over the edge.

The meeting ended with Alex making some weak attempts to thank her for her service. Both knew the damage was done and neither wanted to be where they were at that moment. Sarah went back to her earphones and computer. Alex sat back in his chair and considered the rest of his team.

Leveling with himself, Alex knew that he had assembled a mediocre team. Sarah was the best of the lot. He had two other designers who were generalists. They could create decent brochures, functional websites, and acceptable print ads.

Neither of them excelled at any one discipline. His account directors were equally average. Before joining The Stapleton Agency, Dean Richardson had been an account supervisor at a large local agency. Having been passed over twice for promotion to account director, Dean had been easy prey for Alex to recruit with an offer of becoming an account director at The Stapleton Agency. Alex knew titles were a currency he could afford to be liberal with.

Rhina Sullivan was the other account director at The Stapleton Agency. She was efficient and detail oriented. However, as account director, she was also responsible for client strategy, which was over her head.

Despite having Dean and Rhina (or perhaps because of them), all of The Stapleton Agency's clients wanted to deal with the boss. Alex's name was on the door so he needed to attend virtually all client meetings. Losing Sarah meant his other designers would need to work overtime. He'd need to rely on Dean and Rhina to handle more clients while he spent time recruiting a new designer. His team, average to begin with, would be stretched to their limits.

When he started his agency, Alex dreamt of attracting the best specialized talent in the city, paying them well, building a magical work environment, and eventually selling out to a multinational agency holding company. In reality, he had second-rate generalists working at the beck and call of unknowledgeable clients. It wasn't supposed to be like this.

Alex was tired of the grind and decided it was time to sell his company.

2

A Worthless Business?

Ted Gordon had been a family friend for decades and had inspired Alex to become an entrepreneur. Ted had built and sold a number of businesses over the years and Alex had watched Ted acquire new heights of personal and financial freedom.

Ted was a serial entrepreneur. He had made his first million starting, and ultimately selling, an insurance agency. He had moved on to build a consulting company, which he sold to a multinational firm. He also sold a commercial real estate business a few years ago. By the age of 59, Ted had started, built, and sold five businesses. His net worth was well into eight figures. Not only was Ted a success in business, he was also a success in life. He had a happy family with a beautiful wife and two adult kids who still talked to him. There were also annual ski trips and long summers at the beach house. It seemed like Ted had figured things out, so Alex decided to give him a call.

"Hi Ted. It's Alex."

"Hey, Alex. How are you?"

"I'm okay. Would you mind if I came up to see you? I'd like to get your advice on something I've been contemplating."

Ted's office was on the top floor of a building downtown that overlooked the water. When Alex arrived, a receptionist informed him that Ted would be right out. A few minutes later, Ted came out of his office and put an arm around Alex.

"So I see you've met Cindy. Did she offer you a drink?"

"She did and I'm fine, thanks."

They walked into Ted's office, which had a panoramic, unobstructed view of the water. The office was large—probably 1,000 square feet—adorned with pictures of Ted's family and a hefty oak desk that Alex imagined had been the epicenter of many deals.

They shunned the desk for a more comfortable spot on two white leather chairs divided by a glass coffee table. Ted rested his feet on the coffee table.

"Why did you want to see me?"

Alex knew that he could confide in Ted so he got to the point. "I've decided to sell my business."

"That's a big decision. Let's back up a minute. Why do you think you want to sell?"

Alex recounted the story of First National Bank, Sarah and the rest of his mediocre team, and the company's lumpy cash flow. He talked about how clients always wanted to deal with Alex himself and his agency's dependency on First National Bank. Ted listened carefully, asking questions for clarification.

Having listened to Alex for the better part of 30 minutes, Ted asked a question that seemed somewhat odd. "How would you describe your business to a stranger at a cocktail party?"

Alex thought about this, slightly aggravated to be answering a question Ted knew the answer to already.

"We're a marketing agency. We create marketing materials like brochures, print ads, and websites."

"Who's your competition?"

Alex launched into the list of marketing agencies in town.

"There are other small shops like Reynolds & Harper, Fuel, and Curve Designs. Sometimes we lose out to regional offices of large agencies. There are a lot of freelancers who work from home and . . . "

"So you run a service business highly dependent on one client who in turn demands that you personally tend to their account, and you compete with a lot of other players who provide similar services."

"You could put it that way."

Ted paused a minute before offering his valuation analysis. "Alex, your business is virtually worthless today."

Alex couldn't believe what he was hearing. He'd spent eight years building a business, and the man who he most respected in life and in business proclaimed it to be worthless.

"Are you saying I can't sell my business?"

"No, I'm saying that you can't sell it *today*. If you want to sell it, we need to work on making some changes in your business. I can help, but it won't be easy. You'll need to make some tough decisions and bold changes. Are you prepared to follow my advice?"

"Yes."

"Let's meet here every Tuesday morning at 9:00. In the meantime, I want you to go away and think about what kind of projects you're really good at. Come back next week and we'll talk about what's involved in selling your business."

On his way home, Alex opened his mobile and checked his email. John Stevens had seen the latest round of revisions and had more changes to make to the brochure.

Hostage Taking

Alex got back to the office and took an inventory of projects that needed to get done for the week. In addition to finding a way to placate John Stevens, The Stapleton Agency needed to design and print the *Free Checking* branch posters for First National's retail banking group; redo a website for the largest BMW dealership in town; optimize the website of a local bike shop to improve its natural search ratings; design a logo for a new software company; and write a direct mail package for First National's credit card division. It would be a busy week and Alex needed extra effort from each of his employees.

Tony Martino, The Stapleton Agency's only copywriter, was by all accounts a mediocre writer. Awkward in high school, Tony had chosen a career in advertising because he thought being funny would make him more attractive to the opposite sex. He had been in the bottom half of his class at college and, upon graduation, had bounced around five agencies over three years. On his résumé, Tony characterized his long stretches of unemployment as "freelancing," which was a charitable interpretation of his time spent toggling between video games and online poker. Somehow, Tony had managed to land a short stint at a respected agency in town, so when Alex was desperate for a copywriter, he hired Tony after a 30-minute interview.

Alex was regretting his haste. Tony's most recent copy was the third draft of a direct mail letter intended to promote a new travel rewards credit card being launched by First National

Bank. The draft copy was a string of bad clichés held together with spelling and grammatical errors. Alex drew a large black line diagonally across the page and scribbled *REWRITE* at the top. He tossed the page to the side of his desk and promised himself to get rid of Tony as soon as he could replace Sarah.

The *Free Checking* branch posters were not going to win any creative awards but at least they were done. They needed to be proofed and printed, so Alex sent Elijah Kaplan, his youngest designer, to the print shop for the morning. That left Chris Sawchuk as the only designer to work on the website for Buddy's BMW and the optimization project for the bike store. Chris was reasonably savvy with websites but by no means a specialist. Through some reworking of copy and tags, he had managed to get the bike store ranked fourth among Google natural searches for road bikes and fifth for bike service. The client wanted to be first or second in both categories. Chris broke the news to Alex.

"I can't get them above the fold. I've tried all of my usual tricks and they're still only coming up fourth."

Alex resigned himself to another difficult conversation with a client.

****

Elijah was the son of a marketing manager at First National Bank so Alex had been inclined to hire him six months ago. Word had circulated among the design team that Sarah was leaving and Elijah spotted his opportunity.

"Hey, Alex, do you have a minute?"

"Sure, Elijah, come on in."

Elijah walked into Alex's office and closed the door behind him.

"I've been here six months now and we're stretched pretty thin these days. I've been logging some late nights and I think it's time I get a little bump in my salary."

Alex started counting under his breath so as not to explode. Because his mother worked at First National Bank, Elijah was given a starting salary that was 10 percent higher than was typical for a junior designer. Alex was furious that this little brat had used Sarah's resignation to ask for a raise when he knew full well Alex couldn't refuse.

Choosing his words carefully, he said, "What do you have in mind, Elijah?"

"I think a $5,000 raise would get me to where my peers from design school are. It seems fair under the circumstances."

Alex decided to buy himself some time.

"Elijah, you're a key member of the team and I appreciate the extra work you've been putting in lately. Let's set up a meeting next week where we can sit down for an hour and talk about your progress over the past six months. I'll consider your request and will have an answer when we meet next week."

Elijah, sensing he had his prey on the ropes, agreed.

The Process

Ted greeted Alex warmly and offered him the same leather chair beside the coffee table.

"So how was your week?" Ted asked.

"Brutal," admitted Alex. "My best designer is leaving, I need to find a writer who can write copy for a credit card campaign, a web guy who can decode Google's black box, and my youngest designer wants a raise despite being barely qualified to create a branch poster."

"Sounds like you had a tough week," Ted said. "Did you give some thought to the question I asked you last week?"

Alex had spent time thinking about the types of projects The Stapleton Agency was really good at. He had started by sifting through a file of thank you letters and testimonials from clients. He looked at the time sheets his designers submitted and tracked them back to his most profitable projects. He also thought about the disaster projects over the last year and made a list of the types of projects that caused the most problems.

"It seems the work we're best at is designing logos. We have a system we follow every time we get asked to create a product logo. Clients like the work we produce and we're able to charge a good dollar because clients know a product logo is something they will use for a long time. Once we create one product logo, we have our foot in the door and clients often come back as they launch new products."

Ted considered Alex's conclusion. "Tell me about the system you follow for creating logos."

"It's nothing too formal, but we always start off by asking the client to describe their vision for their product and how they differentiate themselves from their competitors."

Ted began to make notes. "That sounds like a good first step. Let's call it Visioning."

Step 1: Visioning
"What's the next step?" asked Ted.

"After we establish the client's goals, we go through an exercise where we ask the client to personify their product.

For example, we'll ask questions like, 'If your product was a famous actor, who would they be?' and 'If your product was a rock star, who would they be?' One of our favorite questions is a little goofy: 'If your product was a cookie, what kind of cookie would it be?' These questions force the client to think about the personality they want to come through in their logo."

"That sounds unique, Alex. Let's call that Step 2 and give it a name like Personification."

Step 2: Personification
"What's your next step in designing a logo?"

"We then go back to the office and use a pencil and paper to freehand sketch a bunch of ideas. We'll use the business the client is in along with their vision and the personification exercise to come up with a few icons that represent their product."

"Why don't you use a computer for this step?"

"We've found that if you use a computer to show a client rough drafts, they tend to focus on small details they don't like instead of judging the concepts. So by showing them concepts in rough, we force them to focus on high-level ideas instead of details like colors or fonts."

"Let's call this step Sketch Concepts."

Ted updated his notes with the following:

Step 3: Sketch Concepts
"The client will usually like one of the sketches, which then acts as our basis for creating a version on the computer. Again, we limit the variables a client can see by only designing in black and white. That way the client judges the logo on its design merits before we get into colors."

"I've never heard of a design shop doing that—very smart." Ted added a fourth step to his notes:

Step 4: Black & White Proofs
"Once clients like what they see in black and white, we show them color options and they select one. After they select colors, we provide the client with digital files and a brand standard guidebook, and then our work is done."

Ted updated his sheet with the final step in Alex's process:

Step 5: Final Design
"It sounds like you have a five-step logo design process."
Ted angled his notebook so Alex could see what he had written:

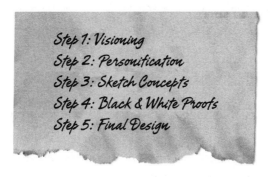

Step 1: Visioning
Step 2: Personification
Step 3: Sketch Concepts
Step 4: Black & White Proofs
Step 5: Final Design

Alex took in Ted's notes and was surprised to see the process they had been following unconsciously for some time suddenly appear on paper.

"What if you focused your business on just doing logos with the Five-Step Logo Design Process?" Ted asked.

Alex immediately recoiled. "There's no way we could build a business on just logos! First National Bank doesn't even use us much for their product logos and they represent 40 percent of our business today. Plus, our other clients think of us as their agency and we get asked to do all sorts of projects for them."

"That's the problem, Alex. You're accepting too many different projects so you need all kinds of different talent on your team. You're a small shop so you have to hire generalists who are inevitably not as good as the specialists the big agencies can hire. So you're asking generalists to perform specialists' work and the results are weak."

TED'S TIP #1	*Being a generalist forces you to hire generalist employees and your offering will be average at best. If you specialize, you can hire specialists and improve the quality of your work.*

"But if we just do logos, we'll have to stop working for First National."

"Alex, relying on First National provides you with some cash flow but it's going to make it very difficult to sell your firm. Nobody wants to buy a business where 40 percent of the revenue comes from one company. It's too risky. If you want to sell your business, you must have a diverse group of clients where no one company makes up more than 10 – 15 percent of your revenue."

TED'S TIP #2	*Make sure that no one client makes up more than 15 percent of your revenue.*

Alex contemplated this advice for a moment and asked for clarification. "So what exactly are you suggesting, Ted?"

"In each business I've sold, we created something I call a Standard Service Offering, which is a consistent process for delivering a service that we focused on at the exclusion of other services. We made sure it was a service clients would need on a regular basis so we could count on recurring revenue. I'm suggesting you become the world's best logo design shop. Write down your five-step process and start talking to prospects about your Standard Service Offering. I'm not asking you to fire your other clients just yet. Start using the Five-Step Logo Design Process with new prospects. Create a one-page description of your approach to creating logos and find 10 people to pitch it to. Come back next week and tell me how you made out."

3

Putting the Process into Practice

Alex scanned the mail—still no check. He closed his office door and considered his cash position. The Stapleton Agency had a payroll of $43,000 per month and monthly rent of $4,000. He needed to come up with at least $47,000 by month's end. There was $68,000 that was 60 – 90 days in arrears, $52,000 of which was one large unpaid invoice issued to First National Bank 65 days ago. The bank usually paid in 60 days. They weren't that late, but Alex's margin for error was slim.

Alex turned his attention to his suppliers. He could delay his trade vendors for an extra 30 days. The phone company would give him an extra month or so. His email to Ralph Stone in the strategic sourcing department of First National Bank was brief, cordial and, Alex hoped, fruitful.

> *Hi Ralph:*
>
> *I hope you're well. I'm inquiring to ensure you received invoice #12-673 in the amount of $52,000. If you have a*

moment, could you please drop me a note to confirm it's being processed?

Thanks in advance,
Alex

Alex hoped for a speedy response.

****

Having done what he could think of to improve cash flow, Alex mulled over his recent conversation with Ted and his outline for the Five-Step Logo Design Process. He had five days to visit 10 prospects. He quickly mocked up a one-page sell sheet and had Chris lay it out and print 10 color copies.

Alex reviewed The Stapleton Agency's Christmas card list and highlighted names he had not spoken with in some time. He fired off two dozen emails and hoped to get at least 10 meetings to pitch his new process.

****

Alex's first two meetings were somewhat awkward as he refined his pitch. His third meeting of the week was with Ziggy Epstein. Ziggy owned Natural Foods Inc., an organic food company that made specialty yogurt and cheese in small batches. Her company supplied most of the specialty food stores in the surrounding area and had used The Stapleton Agency to build a website a few years ago.

Alex met Ziggy at a small office attached to her production facility on the outskirts of town. After getting the pleasantries out of the way, Alex started to probe for a need for his new Five-Step Logo Design Process.

"So, Ziggy, tell me about the new products you're working on."

"We're launching a low-fat version of our yogurt and we're really excited about a new line of organic ice cream we want to launch in the spring."

"The ice cream line sounds like a great extension of your business. Have you come up with a name?"

"Natural Treats Organic Ice Cream."

"That's a great name. Do you have a logo for Natural Treats?"

"Not yet."

Alex spotted his opportunity and launched into his pitch for the Five-Step Logo Design Process.

"Ziggy, it's been a while since we built your website. Including you and your team, we've had the opportunity to work with some great clients over the years. Recently, I did an assessment of all of the projects we've done and came to the conclusion that we're very good at creating logos so we've decided to specialize. We've developed a five-step process for designing logos and have achieved some great results for clients."

With that, Alex revealed his one-page sell sheet and took Ziggy through the process he had mapped out with Ted's help.

"This sounds like a great process. I'd love you guys to work on a logo for our new line of ice cream. Can you send me a proposal?"

****

Alex got back to his office, energized by Ziggy's reaction to the Five-Step Logo Design Process and sat down to write a proposal. Having explained the methodology to Ziggy in person, he only

25

needed to come up with a price tag. Alex started by estimating the number of hours it would take. He looked through the old dockets of logo design projects and estimated the process, with some back and forth for Ziggy's approvals, would take 8 – 12 weeks and generate 35 billable hours for The Stapleton Agency.

Instead of putting his hourly rates in the proposal, Alex decided that, since the project was so well defined, he would gamble and set the price for the Five-Step Logo Design Process at a flat rate of $10,000. The fee was a combination of what he thought a logo was worth, how much agency time it would take, and gut feeling. There was nothing scientific about it.

He emailed the estimate to Ziggy and crossed his fingers.

****

By the end of Friday, Alex had met with six past clients to pitch the five-step process. He was summarizing his findings when he heard the familiar ping of an incoming email. It was a note from Ziggy.

Alex:

Thanks for such a speedy turnaround on the estimate. We'd like to proceed with your proposal. I've attached a signed copy of your estimate as a PDF. Let me know when you'd like to meet for Step 1!

Regards,

Ziggy Epstein
Founder & President
Natural Foods Inc.

Alex pumped his fist and smiled broadly. He had his first client for his new process.

Alex took a celebratory walk around the block. He was basking in the glow of his new assignment when he looked down at his mobile—a missed call. Mary Pradham was trying to reach him.

****

After getting the formalities out of the way, Ted wanted the numbers.

"So how did you make out?"

Alex recounted the results of his test of the Five-Step Logo Design Process. He had sent 24 emails to dormant clients, which resulted in six meetings and one sale to Ziggy.

"Congratulations, Alex, that's great stuff! How did it feel to be talking about your Five-Step Logo Design Process?"

Alex contemplated Ted's question for a minute.

"I felt a lot more confident. In the past, when I was pitching The Stapleton Agency, I felt like I was groveling for table scraps. We didn't specialize in anything so I would take any project they would throw my way."

"And how was pitching the Five-Step Logo Design Process different?"

"When I was pitching our process, I felt like I was an expert. I was in control. I felt confident that we have something of value and I think that confidence was contagious for Ziggy."

Ted smiled. "Good. That's the way it's supposed to feel when you own a product that you control. Alex, I want you to stop thinking of The Stapleton Agency as a service company and start thinking like a product company."

| TED'S TIP #3 | *Pitching a process you own puts you in control.* |

"But designing logos is still a service."

"Fair enough, but your product is your unique methodology for designing a logo. A service company is simply a collection of people with a specific expertise who offer their services to the marketplace. Good service companies have some unique approaches and talented people. But as long as they customize their approach to solving client problems, there is no scale to the business and its operations are contingent on people. When people are the main assets of the business, and they can come and go every night, the business will not be worth very much."

Alex pushed back. "But I've heard of a lot of service company founders who have sold their business."

Ted, sounding more impassioned than at any other point in their meetings to date, stood his ground.

"When a service company is sold, the owners typically get some money up front and the rest of their money is contingent on hitting performance goals in the years ahead. It's called an earn out and often the owners need to stay on for three years or more to get their money. During those three years, a lot can happen that makes it difficult for the owners to meet the acquiring company's performance goals."

Alex was surprised to see such intensity coming from Ted and needed to know more.

"Why are you so against earn outs?"

"In an earn out, you put a significant amount of what your company is worth at risk. The acquiring company is now in

control. An earn out is almost always a disappointment for an
entrepreneur. You've assumed most of the risk and the acquiring company gets most of the reward if you're successful.
Acquiring companies use an earn out formula to buy a business
when they know the founders *are* the business. Your job is to
build The Stapleton Agency up to a point where the business is
independent of Alex Stapleton. That's the only way you can sell
without putting a lot of your compensation at risk in an earn
out. Alex, you need to train people to handle each of the five
steps of your process so you don't have to be the guy piecing
every project together from scratch."

TED'S TIP #4 | *Make the business less dependent on you
so you can reduce or avoid an earn out.*

Then Ted said, "Alex, it looks like something is on your mind.
Tell me what's bothering you."

"I'm committed to transforming my company into something
sellable and I love the Five-Step Logo Design Process but right
now my most immediate concern is cash. I'm expecting a big
check from the bank and they're a little late."

Alex's concerns seemed like music to Ted's ears.

"That's another reason to think of your Five-Step Logo
Design Process as a product. When you have a product, people
expect to pay for it in advance. When you go to Costco to buy
toilet paper, you expect to pay for it before you use it! We're
used to paying for products up front and services after they
have been rendered. Think about the last time you had your

windows cleaned. The service was performed first and then you paid the bill. Products are paid for before you use them. Now that your service has been productized, you need to start charging up front for it."

"I do expect to pay for products up front. If I turn the sell sheet into a brochure and put our fee on the brochure, it would look even more like a tangible product."

Ted brought the conversation back full circle.

"When someone buys a company, they look at the amount of capital they need to tie up to buy the business. If your business is a cash suck—and it sounds like it is today—then they will be willing to pay less for the business. If your business generates cash, they will be willing to pay more to buy your business. Alex, give me a rundown on how you bill for your service today."

"Once an estimate is approved, we get to work on the project. Once we complete the project, we send our bill and wait 60 days or so for a check."

"And how long does a typical project last?"

"That depends on the job, but a logo project usually takes 8 to 12 weeks."

"Alex, I need you to listen very carefully to what I'm about to say. You have a negative cash flow cycle. On a typical logo design project, it takes four to five months before you get paid because it takes two to three months to do the work and another two months before your invoice is paid. The more projects you sell, the more cash you sop up. No wonder your bank is on your case. Now compare your existing cash flow cycle with a model that allows you to charge in advance. You win the project and you ask to be paid before they experience the product.

You then get to use their money for two to three months while you're doing the work. Now imagine that you convince five or ten clients to go through the Five-Step Logo Design Process. Now you have $50,000 or $100,000 of your clients' money to finance your business."

Alex, thinking of the possibilities, smiled for the first time in the meeting.

"The more we sell, the more cash we accumulate. I'll never have to grovel to Mary Pradham again."

"And an acquirer will look at your business as a cash generator instead of a cash suck."

Ted offered his instructions for the week.

"Alex, see how many more clients you can get a meeting with to pitch your Five-Step Logo Design Process. This time, make sure you include the price on the sell sheet and the words 'Billed upon signing letter of agreement'. This is your product and you get to decide how it's billed."

TED'S TIP #5	*Once you've standardized your service, charge up front or use progress billing to create a positive cash flow cycle.*

Alex left Ted's office feeling confident. He knew if he could start getting clients to pay up front, he would get Mary off his case and sleep a lot better at night.

4

Pressure from Within

Tony clutched his latest draft of the direct mail piece for First National Bank as if he was choking it. Alex knew the word *REWRITE* with a diagonal line through his work without further explanation would set Tony off.

"Alex, I need a little more direction if you expect me to be able to write another draft," Tony said.

Alex was at a loss for constructive criticism; he didn't know where to start. It wasn't the opening paragraph or the salutation or the PS or the offer or the tone or the grammar or the spelling. It was everything about the letter that he found unbearable. Quite simply, Alex was paralyzed by Tony's incompetence.

"Look, Tony, I don't have time for this right now. The bank is all over me for their branch posters and I haven't seen Elijah yet this morning. Let's talk about this later."

Tony rolled his eyes and stalked back to his desk.

****

Alex checked in with Sarah to see how she was progressing on what he hoped would be the final changes to John Stevens' brochure project. As he approached Sarah from behind, Alex had a full view of what was on her 21-inch monitor. Instead of the First National Bank brochure, it seemed Sarah was engrossed in a last-minute travel site.

Alex approached, and stood beside Sarah until she noticed him and sheepishly removed her earphones.

"Planning a vacation are we?" Alex asked, the words dripping with sarcasm.

"Alex, I just . . . "

Alex raised his hand like a police officer stopping traffic and walked away without engaging in what he knew would be a feeble excuse.

****

The mail came in and Alex hungrily opened the white number 10 envelopes. There were three invoices from suppliers and two checks. The checks were from small jobs totaling just over $23,000. Better than nothing, but Alex still needed another $24,000 to cover payroll and rent by month's end. He was now down to 12 business days.

****

Alex scheduled his meeting with Elijah for 8:00 a.m.

Elijah walked into Alex's office sporting a smug grin. "Good morning, Alex. How was your night?"

The meeting unfolded as Alex anticipated. Between his mother's job at First National and Sarah's resignation, Elijah squeezed Alex for a raise. Alex countered with Elijah's age and relative inexperience. The result was a split decision with Elijah getting a $2,500 raise and Alex promising to review his salary again in six months.

Elijah would not be working for The Stapleton Agency in six months.

****

Alex scanned his emails and the usual client fires caught his eye: the bike shop wanted a discount on the search engine optimization project because The Stapleton Agency couldn't deliver first or second ranking for their keywords of choice; Buddy's BMW was getting criticism from a lawyer in Munich because their website didn't adhere to BMW's brand standards; and First National's retail banking group wanted another six branch posters printed by the end of the day. Ralph Stone also needed invoice number 12-673 re-submitted with the correct purchase order number listed.

There was an email from Ziggy. She'd enjoyed the Natural Treats personification exercise and was keenly awaiting the sketches as part of step three in Alex's system.

Ziggy's note prompted Alex to put aside the fires in his inbox and turn his attention to developing a new list of prospects to whom he could pitch the Five-Step Logo Design Process.

Gaining Focus

As Alex expected, Ted wanted to start their meeting with a recap of last week's numbers.

"I had eight meetings and Spring Valley Homes agreed to a logo for their new condominium project on the spot."

"That's great progress, Alex."

"In addition to selling a logo to Spring Valley, I also had a good conversation with an old client who asked me for a proposal for a new ad campaign. It would be radio and newspaper ads and possibly a local TV spot."

Ted's face did not reveal his disappointment.

"If you win the new advertising project, when will you receive the cash from the client?"

Alex pondered this for a moment.

"I think the work will take six weeks to produce and this client pays quickly so I should get paid within 30 days."

"So it'll take you roughly 75 days from the day you win the project until the day you get paid?" Ted asked, pausing long enough for the ramifications to sink in.

Alex's enthusiasm waned.

"How much time will you have to commit to writing the proposal?" Ted asked.

"It'll probably take me the better part of an afternoon."

"And if you win the assignment, who will work on the print ads?"

Alex pondered this for a moment. Sarah would be gone by the time the work came in. Elijah was too junior and Chris would be busy with the logos they were already committed to designing. Before Alex could come up with a response, Ted interrupted.

"Look, Alex, if you're going to commit to creating a business that can be sold, you need to commit to offering one process. That means you need to stop accepting other projects."

"But they asked if I would be interested and we could really use the money . . . "

"Clients will test your resolve every day. They're used to bossing their service providers around and, if given the choice, would always prefer you customize your solution just for them. If you want to sell your business, you can't give in. You'll be swimming upstream. Clients will never know you're serious about specialization until you say no to other work. You can't be 'kind of' a specialist. If you're going to be the world's best logo design shop, you can't also sneak in a few ad campaigns. It's why heart surgeons don't attend to broken ankles."

Alex continued to resist.

"But I'm not in much of a position to be turning down work these days."

"An amazing thing will happen when you start turning down other projects in favor of promoting your specialized logo design process—you'll instantly become more referable. If you offer a generic service like advertising or marketing, people will have trouble describing you to their friends and business associates because you are just like everyone else. If, however, you are the world's best logo creators, you'll be memorable and referable. For every advertising project you turn down, you will win a logo assignment."

TED'S TIP #6	*Prove that you're serious about specialization by turning down work that falls outside of your Standard Service Offering. The more people you say no to, the more referrals you'll get to people who do want your Standard Service Offering.*

Alex capitulated. "I'll trust you on this, Ted."

"Good, because the next step is important. As we've discussed, the only way to sell The Stapleton Agency is to make it run without you calling all the shots. That means you need to provide instructions to your employees so that they can implement the Five-Step Logo Design Process."

"Are you talking about some sort of instruction manual?" Alex asked.

"Exactly. Imagine your Five-Step Logo Design Process is an assembly line with five machines and you need to teach someone to operate each machine. Start with how to turn it on, how to make it go, and how to read all of the buttons and gauges as it runs."

Listening, Alex started to jot down notes.

"Take each step in the process and write a detailed instruction manual for completing that step. Give the instructions to one of your team members and see if they can follow the directions. Edit it until someone can follow the instructions without you hovering over them. This week, I'd like you to write an instruction manual for the Five-Step Logo design Process. Bring it with you next time we meet and we can talk about how it is working."

The Instructions

The mail was perched precariously on the corner of Alex's desk. He carefully gathered the pile, cradling it close to his chest so as not to lose anything. One by one, he placed the mail in two piles. The first pile was for junk mail. The second pile contained white number 10 envelopes. The first pile began to grow: a computer flyer, a conference brochure. The second pile started to grow too.

Once he finished sorting the mail, Alex carefully organized the second pile. He took his letter opener, inserted it into the crack at the top of an envelope, and sliced it open. The first envelope revealed an invoice from a photographer they had used for the First National brochure. The next was a $3,400 check. Another invoice. The fourth envelope had First National Bank's familiar blue and gold logo in the top left-hand corner. Alex's pulse quickened. This could only mean one of two things: a) he had received a statement of his accounts from Mary Pradham; or b) the check had arrived. He inserted the letter opener and made a clean incision. With the envelope fully opened he could see inside. It was a check for $52,000.

****

With the check deposited, Alex felt like he could finally breathe again. He sat down with his cup of Grande Bold and wrote down the instructions he wanted followed for each of the five steps in his logo design process.

For step one, he wrote the exact questions he wanted to ask clients. For step two, he outlined which personification examples to use in such painstaking detail that his 83-year-old mother could administer the questionnaire. For step three, the instructions included how many sketches to render and what elements of a client's business to use as inspiration for the imagery in a logo. The fourth step included strict instructions on how to present each black and white version, including the paper stock to use for printing. The fifth step outlined the detailed color combinations to use and what to include in the style guide given to each client.

By 6:00 p.m., Alex had created a first draft of his instruction manual. It was a complete summary of his vision and directions for creating a logo. Now if he could get his staff to follow the instructions, he could extricate himself from personally over-seeing each new logo project.

Alex went home exhilarated by the thought of starting to build some scale into his business.

Employee Mutiny

Alex was slightly nervous as all seven employees of The Stapleton Agency found a seat at the boardroom table. He looked around and sized up his audience. His account directors were sitting next to each other. Rhina was sitting attentively with a notepad and sharpened pencil placed neatly in front of her. Dean sat beside Rhina, fiddling with his BlackBerry and pretending he had important clients to get back to. The designers flocked together on one side of the table with Sarah looking disinterested, Chris thumbing his mobile, and Elijah chatting with Tony. Even Alex's office manager Olga Retzich had been asked to attend this important meeting.

Alex started the meeting by setting the stage for the changes he was about to implement at The Stapleton Agency. He talked about examples of companies that specialize in one thing. He explained why Southwest Airlines only uses the Boeing 737 model of airplane so that their crew can learn one piece of equipment and maintenance teams can quickly spot problems with one set of diagnostic routines to follow. Alex was proud of his example and used it as a springboard into revealing the changes that were afoot at The Stapleton Agency.

Alex read a thank you letter from a client who had used the firm to create a product logo. He also talked about how much more satisfied their logo design clients were when compared to clients overall and how often logo clients returned for multiple logos over time. Alex admitted where they had gotten in over their head taking on advertising projects that went beyond their capabilities.

Alex used a PowerPoint flowchart to reveal the Five-Step Logo Design Process and talked about the work they were doing with Ziggy at Natural Foods. He passed around a copy of the instruction manual that detailed the procedure for each step.

The presentation lasted 45 minutes, and then Alex paused for questions. Rhina was the first to speak.

"I like the idea of specializing in something and getting really good at it."

Chris added, "I'd love to do more freehand sketch work. I haven't done any drawing since art school."

Elijah wasn't so enthusiastic. "Specialization sounds great, but I thought advertising was supposed to be creative. What you're talking about sounds like working in a factory."

Dean chimed in. "I think we should be the trusted marketing advisor for all of our clients. How am I supposed to build a trusting relationship with my clients if all I am doing is flogging one service?"

Sarah, with nothing to lose, said, "As a designer, I don't want to be pigeonholed into having to follow a set of rules."

Elijah had triggered a mutiny. Alex felt his temper rising. He inhaled deeply, counted to five, and said, "Our new process still allows plenty of latitude for creativity."

With that, Alex asked each employee to study the manual and to see him with questions. He quickly adjourned the meeting.

Alex stared as Elijah fumbled to collect his things, refusing to make eye contact with his boss. Anticipating a confrontation, Alex's other employees left the boardroom quickly. Alex walked across the room to close the door.

"Have a seat," Alex said, pointing to a chair.

Sitting back down, Elijah said, "Alex, I didn't mean to . . . "

Alex cut him off. "Why did you become a designer?"

"I was always creative as a kid. I like drawing and did well in art class. It just seemed like a good choice."

"Being creative is a great asset, but The Stapleton Agency is a business. And as a business, our first priority is to make money. If you want to be an artist, I suggest you go find somewhere else to work."

"But Alex, an agency is supposed to be a creative environment."

"Then go work for a traditional agency. We're focused on creating logos using our five-step process."

Elijah sat motionless for more than a minute. Resigning himself to the obvious, he said, "Well, I guess I'm leaving then."

"Good luck."

With that, they shook hands and Elijah returned to his desk. He put a few things in his bag and left.

Alex felt good to have exercised the power he had as the owner of his own company. After all, his name was on the door and he would not stand for such blatant contempt—especially from his most junior employee. The broader implications of what he had just done started to wash over him. He'd be down to one designer. Elijah's mother would find out and that could jeopardize his relationship with First National Bank.

A knock on the door jolted Alex out of his fog. It was Rhina.

"Alex, I know the meeting didn't go as well as you had hoped, but I want you to know I'm really excited about our new focus."

"Thanks, Rhina." Alex said, feeling buoyed by her statement. "I think your skills will be well suited for our new process."

5

The Test

An email arrived from Blair Donaldson and Alex immediately recognized the name as Urban Sports Ware house's chief marketing officer. The subject line read simply: *Congratulations*.

As he opened the note, Alex's mind began to race. He scanned the first few paragraphs and realized The Stapleton Agency had been offered a contract to become the Agency of Record for Urban Sports Warehouse.

****

Alex walked to Ted's office for their regular Tuesday meeting. It had been 24 hours since receiving the email from Blair Donaldson and he needed the exercise to work off the competing messages flying through his brain.

Kicking off the conversation, Alex explained the Urban Sports Warehouse background to Ted.

"A few weeks before we started our regular Tuesday meetings, I responded to an RFP from Urban Sports Warehouse, which is looking for a new agency. I found out yesterday that we've been offered the contract. I know what you're going to say, but this is a huge opportunity for us. It would mean $50,000 per month in steady fees over the next year."

Alex went on to explain the prestige of being the Agency of Record for a big brand like Urban Sports Warehouse. He talked about the awards they could win given Urban Sports Warehouse's appetite for edgy advertising. Ted didn't interrupt; he wanted to give Alex some time to get all his feelings on the table.

Once Alex finished, Ted said, "Alex, why did you come to me for advice on your business in the first place?"

"Because I want to sell my business. Becoming Urban Sports Warehouse's Agency of Record will help that effort tremendously. A lot of the big agencies bid for Urban Sports Warehouse so they'll want to gobble us up to get at the Urban Sports Warehouse business."

"Alex, if you want to work for a big agency for the next five years, then yes, I think accepting the Urban Sports Warehouse engagement could help you sell your company. But the only way a big agency will buy another small, undifferentiated agency will be if they tie you into a five-year earn out agreement. They'll offer you a little bit of cash up front and the rest will be contingent on you achieving milestones they set out for you over the next five years. You'll need to keep and grow the First National account and hang on to Urban Sports Warehouse for the next five years. You'll be answering to a middle manager at a big agency with a lot of rules and procedures of their own. If you miss your targets, they won't be obliged to pay you any more than the small amount of cash you got when you entered into the agreement. You'll be taking all of the risk and will not control the outcome."

Alex contemplated this and wondered if Elijah had already told his mother that her agency had just fired her son.

"My advice continues to be about creating a business that can exist without you. That's the only way you'll sell your company and be able to walk away without being obliged to stick around for five years."

TED'S TIP #7	Generic, owner-dependent service businesses usually sell for no more than a small amount of cash up front and a 3 – 5-year earn out, which places all of the risk on the person selling the business and puts almost all of the potential rewards into the buyer's hands. You need to build a business where the majority of your proceeds get paid up front.

Ted sensed his protégé needed a pep talk.

"You're doing well so far, Alex. You've identified a service that your firm is good at delivering and you've mapped out a repeatable process for delivering it. You've created an instruction manual so others can deliver the service and you're charging up front so that the more you sell, the more cash you will accumulate. I told you your resolve would be tested throughout this process. This is one of those moments. I'm not going to tell you what to do about Urban Sports Warehouse. It's your call."

Alex left Ted's office feeling uneasy. He understood Ted's advice intellectually, but he had aspired to win a client like Urban Sports Warehouse for years. He'd worked so hard on his response to their RFP that it was hard to imagine turning it down.

Opportunity Knocks

Alex reached Blair Donaldson's assistant. She informed him that Mr. Donaldson was finishing a meeting, but that once the meeting adjourned, she'd have him call Alex. The minutes felt like hours as Alex waited. Finally, Blair returned his call.

"Mr. Donaldson thanks for calling back."

"Alex, it's good to hear from you. I'm surprised you didn't call yesterday. We're going to have fun working with you and your team."

"Thanks but . . . " Alex hesitated, summoned his courage, and proceeded. "I have to decline the assignment."

"What are you talking about?"

"Since submitting our proposal to you, we've decided to specialize in creating logos."

"You're a fool . . . you have a tiny agency and we would have made you guys. You better get used to doing business cards for real estate agents because that's the only work you're going to get in this town after I get through telling the members of the AMA about the time you've wasted."

Alex tried to smooth things over.

"I didn't mean to offend you."

The line went dead. Alex looked down to see that he still had plenty of bars on his mobile. Blair had hung up.

****

Alex returned to the office as Dean was preparing to leave for a client meeting. Keen to take his mind off of Blair Donaldson and Urban Sports Warehouse, Alex struck up a conversation.

"Hey, Dean. Off to see the Spring Valley Homes guys?"

"Yup. We're in good shape. We did the personification thing with them last week and I'm going over there right now to show them some concepts."

"Great, mind if I take a look?" Alex asked innocently as he gestured to Dean's zipped portfolio.

"Sure, I guess," Dean said halfheartedly. He left the portfolio closed and started to fumble as he hurried to put on his jacket.

"I'm a little late but I can give you a quick summary. When we got into the personification exercise, it was clear that they have a big vision for this condo project. They want to sell 56 units this fall and make it the first of five condo projects around the city."

"That's great," Alex said, somewhat impatiently. "Can I see the sketches for the logo?"

Dean slowly unzipped his portfolio.

"Instead of just showing them sketches, we decided to show them a little bit more of our creativity." Dean opened his portfolio and revealed a full-color, computer-generated mock-up of a launch campaign. There was a mock-up for a print ad, a brochure, and six logo concepts all printed in full color.

Alex couldn't believe his eyes.

"Dean, where did you get the idea to create this material?"

"I think it's a big opportunity for us and they could turn into a major client."

"Dean, we're focused on logos now."

"Oh sure, I know and I'm presenting six logo concepts as well and . . . "

"Yes, I see that and I also see that the logos are full-color, computer-generated logos, not the black and white sketches that follow the personification exercise in our process. Did you even read the instruction manual I handed out?"

"But Alex, this is a really big client and I just thought it was worth going the extra mile for them."

"I understand but we specialize in logos now and that's all we do. You need to get your head around the fact that we're no longer an agency. Remove the print ad and brochure mock-ups. You can still show them the logo concepts, but next time follow the process and show them black and white sketches first."

Dean rolled his eyes and removed the print ad and brochure mock-ups from his portfolio.

****

As they approached their regular seats, Alex gave Ted the news.

"I turned down the Urban Sports Warehouse assignment."

"You made a good decision."

"I hope so. Urban Sports Warehouse would have been a big client for us."

Ted, sensing a need to restart Alex's enthusiasm for their work together, decided to explain the way they were going to replace and exceed the revenue The Stapleton Agency would have received from Urban Sports Warehouse.

"To sell your business, you need to demonstrate to a buyer that you have a sales engine that will produce predictable, recurring revenue. We need to figure out how many sales reps you need to drive the sales engine and how many companies are in your target market. For now, let's focus on businesses within the city limits. How many companies are there in town?"

Alex had no idea so they went to Ted's desk and huddled around his computer. They found a U.S. Census Bureau website that showed there were 210,000 businesses within a 100-mile radius. Ted wanted to tighten the target market as much as possible.

"Let's assume that to be willing to spend $10,000 on a logo for a new product or division, a business needs to generate at least $1 million in annual revenue."

Alex scanned the site and found the number. "There are 58,000 businesses in the area that do at least $1 million a year."

"Now we need to know how many of those 58,000 companies you can sell a logo to. Think back to when you started selling your Five-Step Logo Design Process. How many companies did you email?"

Alex did the quick math and produced the number.

"I emailed 44 companies."

"And how many of those gave you an appointment?"

"Fourteen."

"And how many logos did you sell?"

"Two so far."

Ted grabbed a pad of paper and scribbled some numbers. He angled the pad so Alex could see his math.

"Your close rate on prospects is 2 of 44, or 4.5 percent. Let's discount that by at least 50 percent because you had a pre-existing relationship with those leads. So let's say your close rate on cold leads is roughly 2 percent. That means the approximate market potential for the Five-Step Logo Design Process, is roughly 2 percent of 58,000, or 1,160 logos. That assumes one logo per company, which is conservative given most companies create logos for new divisions and products on a regular basis. At $10,000 per logo, that's $11,600,000 in market potential here in town. That's a nice little business and we're not even counting how big you could grow if you opened offices in other cities. Nationwide, the business of creating logos could be a $100 million opportunity if you could replicate your model in other cities."

For the first time in the meeting, Alex started to feel better about turning down Urban Sports Warehouse.

"Not only is an acquirer going to want to know how big your business could become, they will also want to know that you have a predictable sales engine that allows you to estimate how many sales you can make. For example, you started with 44 leads and after two weeks you made two sales. That's one logo for each week you were selling. If the average salesperson has 50 productive weeks per year, each salesperson you hire should be able to sell 50 logos. From there we can project out various scenarios. For example, if you want to achieve $1 million in revenue next year, then you need two salespeople. If you think you can handle $2 million in revenue, or design 200 logos, then you need four salespeople."

TED'S TIP #8

Track your conversion rate of pipeline prospects to sales as it will become essential for an acquirer to accurately estimate the size of the market opportunity.

"An acquiring company will want to see the model for your sales engine, including how many opportunities you have and your historical close rate, to estimate the size of the market opportunity. You need to demonstrate you know your sales engine and that you can predict, with a fair degree of accuracy, how your sales engine will perform under their roof. Most importantly, you need to demonstrate that you're not the only one who can sell logos."

"But I don't have any sales reps," Alex reminded Ted.

"I know. You need to hire at least two."

"Why two? Shouldn't I start with one?"

"Salespeople are competitive and they will compete with each other, which will allow you to prove that your sales engine is not just dependent on one good sales rep. Besides, you have payroll and rent that amounts to roughly $600,000 per year so you need to sell at least $1 million of logos this year to cover your costs and show some profit this year."

TED'S TIP #9	*Two sales reps are always better than one because they compete with each other and prove to a buyer that you have a scalable sales model (not just one good sales rep).*

Alex started doing the math and it didn't add up.

"If I hire two sales reps, won't my payroll and rent add up to more like $700,000 or $800,000?"

"Yes, if you keep all of the staff that you have now. Spend some time this week thinking about the team you need to administer the Five-Step Logo Design Process. I bet you'll find one or two staff members that you no longer need."

As Alex left Ted's office, he knew he was in for some difficult conversations in the coming week.

6

The Candidates

Firing Tony Martino was an easy decision—Tony was a bad writer to begin with and Alex didn't need a copywriter to administer the Five-Step Logo Design Process. He could always use free-lancers for the odd copywriting job the bank handed down. The conversation was quick. Tony was expecting it and Alex treated him fairly.

The conversation with Dean was a little more difficult. Alex tried to soften the blow by describing the strategic projects he could work on at a larger agency and how many of Dean's talents would go unused at The *new* Stapleton Agency. Dean left in a huff.

Shedding Tony and Dean saved The Stapleton Agency $125,000 a year. Alex decided not to immediately replace Sarah, saving the firm another $70,000 per year. He'd found enough cuts to hire two intermediate salespeople without increasing his overall cost base.

****

Blake Worthington had returned from two weeks at his family's summer house. He wore a blue suit over his 6'2"-frame. His crisp white shirt was held together at the sleeves by gold cufflinks, which clinked against a Rolex his father had given him upon graduation from The Cheshire Preparatory Academy. White teeth created the perfect contrast to the golden tan he had cultivated over the fortnight away. His Windsor knot was carefully assembled and his full head of blonde hair had been molded into place.

Blake was one of four candidates Alex had short-listed for the newly created sales roles at The Stapleton Agency. They shook hands and started with some easy banter.

Alex scanned Blake's résumé. After Cheshire, Blake had attended Cornell. After graduation, there was a six-month trip to Southeast Asia where he had learned to kite surf, after which he returned to the U.S. and took his current job. For the past two years he had served as a junior member of the business development team at one of the big advertising agency conglomerates.

"Why do you want to work for The Stapleton Agency?"

Blake, trying to anticipate what he thought Alex wanted to hear, said, "A big agency is a great placed to be trained but I want to start seeing the direct results of my work."

"How do you like the advertising business so far?"

Blake sat up in his chair, sensing an opportunity to impress Alex.

"I love the power of a brand. I like understanding the core attributes of a brand and finding a way to express those creatively through a variety of different media. I'm a huge believer in integration. They say TV is dead but if you want to build a brand you can't beat the reach of TV."

The interview unfolded predictably with Alex lobbing softball questions and Blake hitting them out of the park with easy clichés and rehearsed pap he had read in a book titled *How to Land Your Dream Job*. It ended with Alex promising to be in touch the following week.

Alex was impressed with Blake's polish, pedigree, and big agency experience and thought he would represent The Stapleton Agency well. He put a large check mark on Blake's résumé and filed it with the other candidates still in the running.

****

Back at his desk, the usual fires were smoldering in his inbox. John Stevens wanted to meet with Alex tomorrow to go over a Spanish version of the brochure. Olga wanted to know if she could renew the lease on the photocopier. Sarah wanted a reconciliation of the vacation pay she was owed. Then Alex saw Ziggy's name with the subject header *Thanks*. He opened the note and read it:

Alex:

I want to let you know how happy we are with the logo your team created for Natural Treats. I just met with Rhina this morning and she took me through the color versions of Chris' design. It looks good and I have already distributed your brand standard guidebook to all of our staff. Rhina was very efficient and moved the project along well. Chris is a creative guy and a pleasure to work with. I'll know who to call for our next product launch. Thanks again,

Ziggy Epstein

Founder & President
Natural Foods Inc.

Alex was ecstatic. It always felt good to get a thank-you letter from a client but typically the letters praised Alex personally for his creativity and thoughtfulness. Ziggy's letter was special because it recognized his team. For the first time, Alex felt like he was building a business that was more than just Alex Stapleton.

Based on Rhina and Chris' work on the Natural Treats logo, Alex put them in charge of the Five-Step Logo Design Process. Rhina would conduct step one, the visioning exercise, and step two, the personification interviews. Chris would be responsible for step three, the sketch, and the computer-generated renditions of steps four and five. Rhina would write and present the brand standard guidebook and manage the client throughout the process. Alex had a system and people to oversee its delivery. Now all he needed was a sales team.

****

Angie Thacker dressed conservatively for her interview with Alex. Her hair was pulled back and fell neatly over the shoulders of her dark blue suit.

Alex reviewed her résumé. After college at a state school, Angie landed a job selling mobile phones at a local wireless retailer. She'd been the top salesperson at the store and, after two years selling phones, she had taken a job selling yellow pages advertising for one of the big phone companies. She had quickly risen to be among the top 10 percent of sales reps nationally.

"Why do you want to work for The Stapleton Agency?"

"I love selling and I understand you're just starting a sales team at The Stapleton Agency. I'd love to help you build a professional sales team from the ground up."

"What makes a salesperson professional?"

"The key to my success in sales has always been working my numbers. I know how many meetings I need to close a sale. I know how many sales I need to hit my quota for the week and how that rolls up to help me make my month, my quarter, and my year. It all starts with knowing how many meetings I need to schedule each week and it flows from there."

Alex couldn't believe how scientifically Angie had broken down her goal setting. Intrigued, Alex wanted to know more.

"What motivates you, Angie?"

"I'm a competitor. I love to win."

The interview continued with Alex feeling like he was at the zoo peering at a foreign animal. Growing up in the creative business, Alex had always been around creative people. He'd never met anyone so disciplined, or with such a linear thought process.

Alex said goodbye to Angie with a promise to respond with a decision next week.

The Jibe

Tuesday morning, Ted called Alex on his mobile to see if he wanted to go for a sail and have their talk on the boat instead of Ted's office. The forecast called for a 15 – 20 knot onshore wind. They agreed to meet at Ted's yacht club.

Although he could afford a much larger vessel, Ted loved the thrill of sailing a small boat on big water so had opted for a Laser 4000. Helping Ted rig the boat, Alex outlined his progress since they'd last met. He described how he had made room on his payroll for two salespeople by letting Tony and Dean go and not replacing Sarah. He also described the candidates he was interviewing for the sales roles. He spent the majority of the time contrasting Blake and Angie. Both had left a positive impression on Alex for different reasons and Alex tried to articulate that for Ted.

"Blake understands service businesses. He's worked for an agency for two years and knows the creative world. He understands selling intangibles."

Ted listened intently while hoisting the sails and making his way out of the harbor. While looking at the direction of the wind, he kept probing Alex.

"Tell me about Angie."

"Angie is completely different. She knows nothing about the marketing industry and she has spent her entire career selling tangible products that a prospect can touch and feel. Angie is all process and systems and she is extremely goal oriented."

Ted probed further. "Sounds like you have two very different candidates. How about the rest of the people you interviewed?"

Alex thought for a moment. "You could put them into two categories: people like Blake who have a background selling services and people like Angie who have sold tangible products."

With his eyes scanning the horizon, Ted gave Alex the benefit of his experience.

"I think you need to avoid Blake like the plague and hire a team full of Angies."

Alex was surprised at Ted's conviction.

"How can you be so sure? Blake went to Cornell, his father knows a number of the CEOs in town, and he works at one of the top agencies in the country."

"In my experience, people like Blake, who are used to working in a service business, are good at consultative selling. They ask a lot of open-ended questions and probe for a client's need. The clients reveal their innermost fears and then expect people like Blake to custom-tailor a solution. Blake will try to convince you to tailor the Five-Step Logo Design Process to meet the unique needs of each client."

"So why are you so sure Angie will work out?"

"From what you've told me about Angie, she will be fantastic. You have one process and you have packaged it to look like a product with five steps that don't change from one client to the next. Product salespeople are used to doing the mental gymnastics required to position their product to meet the needs of their prospect. A product salesperson doesn't have the luxury of changing their company's product every time they hear a need from a customer. They need to position the product they're stuck with to meet the customer's needs. That's exactly the kind of person you want selling the Five-Step Logo Design Process."

Alex took this in slowly. They sped along the water as the wind picked up.

"That sounds counterintuitive to being a service provider."

Ted, not deterred by the wind speed and the increasing angle of the Laser, yelled back, "It is! Again, most service companies are not sellable other than for a long, risky, and painful earn out. They depend on their owners to be the rainmakers. When the owner goes, there is no more business and acquiring

59

companies understand that. You need to stop doing the selling yourself and hand the reins to a team of people like Angie."

TED'S TIP #10 | *Hire people who are good at selling products, not services.*

They sped toward the outer bay where the waves were picking up. After a long silence, Ted upped the ante in their work together. "Alex, the next step in the process is going to take enormous courage on your behalf. Are you ready?"

"It can't take any more courage than sailing with you," Alex said, half joking.

"It's time you tell your existing clients that you will no longer be able to support their adverting needs because you are specializing in logo design."

Alex immediately calculated the implication of Ted's direction.

"Can I keep doing other work for First National Bank?"

Ted was emphatic. "Absolutely not."

Alex reminded Ted of the financial impact of what he was suggesting and Ted stood his ground.

"Alex, you can't be half-pregnant. If you keep doing other work that falls outside of your logo design process, you'll send mixed messages to all of your stakeholders."

"Ted, First National Bank accounted for 40 percent of our revenue last year."

"I know and your business is unsellable as a result. If you keep offering custom services, you'll need to replace your senior designer and your copywriter and you'll telegraph to the market that you're not committed to your logo design process. First National refuses to deal with anyone but you so if you did sell, you'd be locked in for years. If a client is given the choice, they would always rather have a custom-tailored solution just for them. So if you run a custom service business in parallel to your logo design business, you won't be giving the Five-Step Logo Design Process a chance to thrive."

"I'll need to think about that," Alex said.

"I warned you that you would need courage to take this step."

Out of the blue, Ted gestured for Alex to look down at the tiller in Ted's hands.

"I'm asking you to make a 180-degree turn in the way you think about your business. It's a little bit like a jibe," and with that, Ted pulled the tiller hard toward him. The boat careened downwind and keeled over at what seemed to Alex like an impossible angle. The boom followed the boat's turn and swung violently from one side of the boat to the other. Ted pushed Alex over to the other side of the boat while he pulled in the sail and positioned himself next to Alex. The wind filled the sail with a 'thwack', Ted hiked out so that his feet were on the gunnels, and the boat started speeding for shore.

TED'S TIP #11 | *You can't be "kind of" a specialist. Either you specialize or you don't. Stop taking projects that fall outside of your Standard Service Offering.*

"To jibe properly, you need to throw the tiller all the way to one side. There's a moment when you feel a little out of control just before the sail flips sides and starts catching wind on the other side of the turn. You can't half commit. If you don't throw the tiller all the way across, you'll never turn the boat and you'll end up in the water. I'm asking you to jibe The Stapleton Agency."

7

Growing Pains

Angie's first week at The Stapleton Agency was productive. Alex asked her to divide the prospect list into four territories based on quadrants of the city. Angie recommended one of her former colleagues from her time at the yellow pages directory to join Angie as the second sales rep. Based on her recommendation, Alex met with Seamus O'Reilly.

Seamus was also in the top 10 among sales reps at Angie's former company. The two had worked together and enjoyed the friendly competition of jostling for the top spot each month. In Seamus, Alex saw a lot of the same attributes he valued in Angie. He hired Seamus without hesitation.

Two weeks later, Seamus started at The Stapleton Agency. His first project was to erect a whiteboard in the middle of the office that detailed both sales reps' weekly sales statistics. Each day, they updated their number of appointments confirmed for the week and the number of logos sold. They each had a goal of one logo per week.

By the fourth week of selling, Angie was consistently setting up 10 appointments per week. Seamus was up to eight appointments per week. Finally, on the last Friday of the month, Angie sold her first logo. She raced into Alex's office with the signed contract. They both celebrated by smashing the bell Angie and Seamus had set up outside Alex's office. The entire agency heard the commotion and got up from their desks to join the celebration.

Alex beamed all the way home that night. Not only had he built a process others could deliver but someone else other than Alex could sell it. It occurred to him as he pulled into his garage that he didn't even know the name of the company Angie had sold her first logo to. He reveled in the feeling of building something larger than himself.

****

The next week Seamus sold his first logo and Angie sold another. They were both consistently landing 10 new appointments per week. Alex got into the habit of checking the board every day and cheering his team on. By the end of the fourth week of selling, Angie had sold five logos and Seamus had sold four.

****

Alex agreed to meet with John Stevens at his office to discuss the Spanish version of First National's new brochure. He rarely wore a suit but for some reason decided to wear one for this occasion.

They exchanged pleasantries and John launched into a description of the changes he required for his brochure to ensure its suitability for the Hispanic market. Alex listened carefully. By the time he issued his last directive, John was collecting his things, signaling he was finished with him. Alex knew that it was now or never.

"John, it's been a pleasure working with you over the last few years. In fact, we've worked on a lot of different projects together. The logo we designed for the wealth management division last year stands out for me. Do you remember that project?"

"Of course, you guys did a great job. Listen Alex, I've got another meeting so . . . "

"This will only take a second, John. The logo we did for your wealth management division was not unusual for us. In fact, we have had great success designing logos for a lot of clients. So much so, that we have decided to specialize in creating logos."

"That's great, Alex. When can I see the first draft of the Spanish version of the brochure?"

"John, we'll get you the first version of the brochure next Monday but this will be the last brochure we create for you. The trade-off for specializing in logo design is that we won't be able to accept other types of projects going forward."

"But Alex, First National Bank gives you tens of thousands of dollars of work every month. I'm not sure you're in a position to dictate to us."

"I understand, John, and I appreciate the support you have given us, but that's the decision we've made and I hope we can continue to work together when you have new products to launch that need a logo."

"I have to say I'm disappointed. I mean, I applaud your focus, but I thought we were a special client."

"You are a special client, which is why I wanted to tell you in person."

Alex felt good about his decision. He had stood his ground and left John's office walking tall for the first time.

The Sacrifice

Harry Stumberger had been Alex's accountant since he started The Stapleton Agency. Each quarter, Harry spent two days at the office. Harry worked with Alex's office manager Olga to ensure that collections were on track and that taxes were being paid on time. Harry would review the invoices Olga had produced and the expenses they had incurred, after which Harry would issue a profit & loss statement that detailed the agency's affairs for the previous three months.

Harry was scheduled to meet Alex at 10:00 a.m. and, as usual, Harry arrived early. He stumbled into Alex's office fighting with his umbrella. Alex was huddling with Angie and Seamus reviewing the latest numbers on the whiteboard and called out to Harry as he arrived.

"Hey, come on in, Harry. Make yourself at home. I'll be in my office shortly."

Harry settled in by removing a pad of paper, pencil, and sharpener from his briefcase. He also extracted a laptop computer and a large blue file.

Five minutes later, Alex entered the office.

"Thanks for coming. How are we doing this quarter?"

Harry hesitated and then decided to tell it to Alex straight.

"Not well. You're on target to lose $12,000 this month and, unless things turn around, another $9,000 next month."

"How's that possible, Harry? We've been selling logos like crazy and we have a ton of cash in the bank."

"Your cash position is the one bright spot, but selling those logos is killing your business."

"I'm confused."

"For each logo you sell, you bill $10,000 up front, which is great for your cash flow. Unfortunately, according to generally accepted accounting principles, or GAAP, I need to apply that revenue in three equal installments starting with the month you sell it and ending three months later. That means I can only recognize $3,333.33 of the $10,000 you bill for a logo project this month. You've gone from recognizing the revenue from projects in the month you win them to recognizing revenue across three months. It is having the effect of cutting your monthly revenue by two thirds on paper."

"So we're going to lose money this month?"

"Yes, and next month too unless you start accepting other projects again. And if this keeps up, you can forget about declaring a bonus this year. You'll be lucky to break even by the end of the year."

Alex listened to Harry and cursed Ted in his mind. He knew he should have accepted the Urban Sports Warehouse project.

****

Alex flicked the wipers on high speed and just made out the entrance into Ted's underground parking garage through the rain. It was Tuesday and the combination of the rain and his meeting with Harry had dampened Alex's mood.

The effervescent Cindy took his coat and provided a bright spot in Alex's morning. Ted was finishing up on the phone and waved Alex in. He took his normal spot on the big white leather chairs in front of the coffee table in Ted's office. Ted came over, greeted Alex, and asked for his regular update.

"Give me the numbers."

"Both Angie and Seamus are consistently getting eight to ten appointments per week. Angie closed five logos last month and Seamus closed four so they are both tracking well against their goal of one logo per week each."

"That's great news, Alex. You must be thrilled."

"Yes and no. I met with Harry last week and he gave me some disturbing news."

"And what did Harry have to say?"

"Harry said I should have accepted the Urban Sports Warehouse contract."

"Of course he did. Alex, Harry is paid to count the numbers. He does not have the context for what we are doing. He has no way of distinguishing from the good, scalable revenue you get from selling logos and the bad, one-off revenue you get from projects. To Harry, it's all just revenue. Since your Five-Step Logo Design Process takes three months to deliver, he's legally obliged to account for that revenue on your profit & loss statement across three months. As you move from ad hoc project work to a single productized service, there will be a point where, on paper, you're in trouble. Let me ask you: How does your bank account look?"

"We have a lot of cash because we billed for all of the logos we sold up front. I'm surprised Mary hasn't called to invite me to lunch."

"While you're in the midst of making this change, you will show a loss on paper and that's okay as long as your cash flow remains strong and you keep selling logos. In three months, you'll start entering months with revenue on the books from logos you sold this month. You will be starting each month with a base of revenue and adding to it with each logo sold. You need to sacrifice for the next three months until your paper statements catch up with the progress you're making."

"But my fiscal year closes in two months and I was planning to declare a bonus this year to pay off my mortgage. There won't be much profit for me to take out of the company."

"That's true, Alex. You'll probably need to trim your bonus this year. But think of this as very mild short-term pain for a very big gain down the road. If we can get someone to buy your business, you will be able to pay off 10 mortgages. It's worth taking a small hit this year."

TED'S TIP #12

Ignore your profit & loss statement in the year you make the switch to a Standard Service Offering and ensure that your partners and spouse are prepared to forgo a bonus in the year you make the switch. Make your cash flow statement your most important day-to-day management report in the year you make the switch.

"How am I supposed to sell a company without any profit?"

"Alex, creating a sellable business takes time. You're going to have to stick with me for the long haul."

"How long a haul are we talking?"

"I need you to give me two more years."

"Two years is a long time, Ted."

"Yes, but you've been running The Stapleton Agency for eight years. Wouldn't it be worth investing another two to finally get rewarded for all of your hard work? Besides, if you sold the business tomorrow, and I'm skeptical we could even find a buyer, they would only agree to buy your company if you signed on for a five-year earn out. I'm really asking you for a two-year commitment as opposed to five. I'm actually going to save you three years."

"When you put it like that, I guess I can't refuse. I was getting excited about the prospect of selling and spending some more time with Pam and the kids. You know, Jenny will be entering high school this year and Max is right behind her. I only have a few more years before they're off to college."

"I understand, Alex. The next two years will be hard work but they will also be much more enjoyable. Your cash flow will be strong. You will no longer be the 'go-to guy' for every client, which will reduce the number of client headaches you have. You'll probably be able to take some vacation time with the family. I think you'll find the next two years to be a lot more fun than the last two and you will be able to have confidence in the fact that you're building something sellable."

TED'S TIP #13	*You need at least two years of financial statements using the Standard Service Offering model before you sell your company.*

****

Pam Stapleton had been married to Alex for 14 years. She'd encouraged Alex to start The Stapleton Agency and had been his greatest cheerleader over the years. But that was before the kids, the orthodontist bills, and the mortgage. Now Pam had grown used to the bonus checks Alex brought home.

Alex knew he would need to start gently.

"Honey, I need to talk to you about the work I've been doing with Ted Gordon."

"Great, I've been meaning to ask you about your Tuesday sessions."

"We've made a lot of progress, but we're at a critical stage now and it's going to have an impact for us personally this year."

"What exactly are you talking about?" Pam said, hesitating.

"We're making some changes so that my business will be sellable in the long term. But in the short term, I'll make less money on paper this year. That means I won't be able to declare a bonus."

"But Alex, you promised we'd pay off the mortgage this year and we told the kids we'd take them to Hawaii for spring break. We don't have the money for that trip just lying around."

"I know and we can still go on vacation but we'll just have to pick somewhere less expensive this year. We need to make some sacrifices this year but, if we do this right, I'll be able to sell my business and then we can take a lot more family vacations down the road."

Alex hugged his wife and promised himself he would make it up to her.

The Number

Over the next few months, life at The Stapleton Agency found a steady rhythm. Angie and Seamus continued to sell roughly one logo each per week. Rhina enjoyed having a system to follow and Chris was getting efficient at creating logos. The clients of The Stapleton Agency were for the most part satisfied with the results. Olga continued to march off to the bank every Friday afternoon with more checks to deposit. Things were going well enough for Alex to take a day away from the office to do some thinking.

****

Alex inhaled the salt in the cool air as he stepped out of the car. Waves were breaking on shore as he walked along a path leading to the ocean. The trail cut through a tall sand dune that rose up more than 60 feet high on both sides. As the path turned south, the beach house came into view. It sat on its own with the next clos-est house at least 500 feet down the beach. The entire structure was enclosed by windows, which reflected the sun as it rose in the east. The November morning meant that the beach was deserted. Alex imagined the hive of activity that must take place on a warm August afternoon.

It was off-season and none of Ted's family were using the beach house so he had offered it to Alex for his planning session. Alex surveyed his home for the next 24 hours. He started in what appeared to be the family room. It was large with modern furniture positioned to take in the sunrise.

He opened a large set of double doors to discover what he assumed was the master bedroom and made his way to the bed, removed his shoes, and lay on the king-sized bed, imagining waking up to the sun rising over the horizon. A small teak table on the patio off the master bedroom separated two steamer chairs. In addition to the expansive master quarters, there was a doorway leading to a bathroom with a two-headed steamer shower and heated slate floors.

Off the kitchen there was a set of double doors, which opened onto a deck that stretched out for 30 feet and ran the circumference of the house. The hot tub crafted into the cedar was big enough for 12 people. He sized up the stainless steel Weber and determined that it had the perfect cooking surface for the 10-ounce filet resting in the fridge. This was going to be a good day.

Ted agreed to lend Alex his beach house on the condition that Alex use some of the time to answer a simple question. Ted had written the question on a piece of paper and sealed it inside a small envelope, which he instructed Alex to open only after he got to the beach house. Intrigued, Alex opened the envelope. Inside was a single recipe card with a handwritten question scribbled on one side:

Alex:
What is the price at which you would be prepared to sell The Stapleton Agency?
Ted

The number.

It was a question Alex had thought about a lot over the past eight years.

To answer the question, Alex thought about it from a variety of angles. First he asked himself what the business would be worth to someone else. With his year-end approaching next month, Harry had given him a preliminary snapshot of how he would likely end the year financially:

Revenue:	$1,400,000
Expenses:	$1,313,000
Pre-Tax Profit:	$87,000

Alex understood small service businesses like his typically sell for roughly 3 – 4 times pre-tax profit, which meant his business was worth less than $500,000. It wasn't enough.

Then he came at Ted's question from a different angle: What was the business worth to him? How much money did he need to feel free? The second number was a lot bigger. Given the wide gap between the two numbers, Alex decided to move on to the rest of his planning agenda but resolved to have Ted's question answered before he left the beach house.

He spent the rest of the morning planning the year ahead. He thought about the financial performance he would need to attract a buyer and knew that he had to significantly increase both his top and bottom line.

Angie and Seamus were reliably selling one logo each per week. They charged $10,000 per logo so they would likely sell a little less than $1 million worth of logos. He scribbled numbers on a pad and played with various scenarios. He had confidence that he could find more salespeople but also wanted to balance what Rhina and Chris could deliver. The Five-Step Logo Design Process was somewhat new, yet he definitely wanted to grow. He settled on a goal of $2,500,000 in annual revenue and made a note that he would need to hire three more salespeople, as well as a new account director and designer to help Rhina and Chris manage the load.

Next, he turned his attention to his expenses. A pre-tax profit of 15 percent or $375,000 was a reasonable goal given that he didn't have any hard costs associated with the business of creating logos. He went through his expenses line by line, looking for costs to cut to make his profit margin goal achievable. He vowed to drop his subscription to *Advertising Age* given that he no longer offered advertising. There was no need for freelance copywriters and he didn't need to attend the American Association of Advertising Agencies' annual media conference in San Diego this year since he no longer bought media for his clients. He was pleasantly surprised at the costs he could cut out of the company given his focus on logos. The 15-percent margin number seemed reasonable even with three extra salespeople and help for Rhina and Chris.

The morning had been a success and Alex rewarded himself by tucking into the sandwich he had brought with him from the city. After lunch, Alex walked down the beach. As he made his way down the beach, Alex's mind wandered back to Ted's question: How much was eight years' work worth to Alex? How much was realistic? The questions kept coming and Alex was no closer to an answer for Ted.

The rest of the afternoon was spent back at the beach house thinking through the changes Alex would need to make to support revenue of $2,500,000.

****

The Weber's automatic starter responded after just one depression of the knob. Alex put the grill on high and let it warm up for five minutes. He opened the bottle of Beringer he had bought and poured a glass but did not drink, opting instead to let the wine open up and embrace the sea air. With the grill at 400 degrees, Alex seared both sides of the meat and cooked it for five minutes. Dinner was ready.

He sliced a thin layer of steak and inspected the color—a perfect shade of pink. It tasted as good as it looked and he washed his first piece down with a hearty mouthful of Beringer. He closed his eyes and savored the explosion of taste as the wine embraced the steak.

Eating alone, Alex smiled and reflected on the progress he had made so far in working with Ted. Groveling for work from First National Bank had been replaced by a steady stream of new customers; personally juggling the management of all of the clients had been replaced by Rhina following the instruction manual; and late night calls to Mary Pradham had been replaced by figuring out how to invest his extra cash. His mind again turned to Ted's question. He poured himself another glass of California's finest. Perhaps encouraged by the wine, he decided to suspend the reality of what he thought his business was worth today and instead thought about how much money he would need to lead the life he dreamed of.

There were the requisite things he wanted, but overall he was surprised by how modest his material needs were. He liked his car. His house would need to be paid off. A beach house would be nice but not necessary. Maybe some travel with Pam and the kids. In all, his lifestyle needs were not that demanding. What he really craved was freedom. He had spent his working life at the beck and call of clients and was tired of having others tell him what to do. He wanted to feel free of needing to work. With the wine anesthetizing the reality of what his business was actually worth, Alex answered Ted's question.

He wanted to sell The Stapleton Agency for $5 million.

8

The Number

Alex felt a rush of satisfaction as he piloted the Range Rover back into the city. The big V8 engine easily handled 60 miles an hour and hardly sounded like it was working at 2,000 RPM. It was still early so, after a quick stop for a Grande Bold, Alex headed directly to Ted's office to drop off the keys to the beach house.

Ted was getting off the phone and gestured to Alex to wait for him. The call ended and Alex handed Ted the keys.

"Thanks, Ted. Your place is fantastic."

"Glad you liked it, Alex. How did the planning go?"

"Good. I'm going to try to hit $2,500,000 dollars of revenue this year and I'd like to improve our profit margin to 15 percent pre-tax."

"Those would be significant improvements over where you are today. Did you open the envelope?"

"I did."

"So, what's your number?"

Surprised by Ted's lack of tact, Alex paused.

"First I came at it from the point of view of what I thought the business was worth. Then I looked at our goals and then . . . "

Ted listened patiently as Alex tried to explain his rationale.

"I thought about the work I've put into the business to date, how much more work is left to get done over the next two years, and . . . "

Alex was nervous about revealing his number to Ted. He looked up, hesitated a moment, and then said, "I want to get $5 million for my business."

Ted didn't flinch at hearing Alex's number. Instead, he offered a simple directive.

"I want you to do something for me. It may not be immediately clear why you need to do this today but trust me, it will become clear down the road and you'll be glad you did. Take one of these recipe cards . . . " Ted handed him a card like the one he had used to write his question for Alex to consider at the beach house " . . . and write down $5 million on this card. Then put it in this envelope and seal it."

"Sounds cryptic. Why do I need to write it down?"

"That will become clear later. Just write it down and put the envelope where you'll be able to find it in a couple of years."

****

Angie and Seamus continued to sell well through December. Despite the holidays, Angie sold six logos and Seamus sold five. He asked both Angie and Seamus to recommend sales-people they knew from their previous jobs. One of his friends had heard Seamus bragging about his new company and had expressed an interest in joining. Alex hired him after a short interview. Angie recommended a friend who was returning to the workforce after taking a couple of years away to start a family. Alex got the word out among his contacts and found the fifth sales rep he needed.

They helped their new colleagues get familiar with the selling system they had designed. In the meantime, Alex put the word out to his network that he was looking for a new account director. He interviewed six people looking for someone with Rhina's attention to detail. He hired Belinda Carter away from a rental car agency where she had been thriving as a branch manager. Rhina and Belinda hired a coordinator to help with some of the details.

Alex contacted his alma mater where he had attended art school and let the professors know he was looking for designers who could freehand sketch and use the latest computer design programs. He asked Chris to meet with a few designers and collectively they picked out a designer that met their criteria.

The Stapleton Agency was growing: Five salespeople, two account directors, two designers, one coordinator and Olga managing the office and the books.

****

The snow fell all night, making the morning drive to the office slower than usual. Alex parked in his usual spot and trudged through the slush to the building and stepped inside. He shook off the snow and salt as best he could and made his way to his office. Angie was waiting for him leaning against his doorway. She stepped aside to let Alex in.

"Alex, can we talk for a few minutes?"

"Sure, Angie, let me just get my coat off . . ."

Angie didn't waste any time.

"I'm glad we brought in three new sales reps but I'm getting stretched thin. They have a lot of questions and I want to be helpful but I'm getting to a point where my sales are starting to suffer. I know Seamus feels the same way."

Alex tried to ease Angie off the ledge. "Angie, I know you've been really helpful at bringing the new guys up to speed and I appreciate all the extra time you've invested."

"That's great, but I think we're at a point now where you need to decide if you want me to sell or manage. I can't do both."

Alex agreed to get back to Angie with a resolution to her concerns next week.

****

The last Tuesday of the month started as most other Tuesdays had in the past six months with Alex offering Ted the week's numbers.

"February has been a good month so far," Alex reported. "Angie closed four logos, Seamus is at five for the month, and the new sales reps each sold their first logos."

"Alex, that's great news!"

"Yes, but our growth is starting to create some problems. Angie spends a lot of her time teaching the new sales reps our process. I know Rhina is feeling stretched as Belinda gets up to speed and Chris has already said we need a third designer."

"Good," Ted said. "It's about time you built a management team."

"Sounds like something First National would have."

"If you're going to sell your business, you need to demonstrate that it can run without you. You need to show a potential acquirer that you have a management team that can keep the business running when you're gone."

"Are you suggesting I bring in outside managers?"

"Not at all. Sounds like Angie, Rhina, and Chris are already your managers. You just need to make it official."

"I guess you're right. But isn't that going to be expensive?" Alex protested.

"Not necessarily," said Ted. "You need to align their compensation with your goals. You can do that with a small bonus and give them a chance to share in the growth of The Stapleton Agency."

"Are you talking about sharing equity with them?"

"Sharing equity can get messy. It's time consuming, and why dilute your equity and complicate things when you don't have to."

"So if not with equity, how else can I let them participate in our growth?"

"There are a lot of options," Ted explained. "You have to decide if you want to reward loyalty, in which case you might create a stay bonus tied to them being employed at some date in the future. Alternatively, you could create a performance bonus for achieving certain targets."

"What did you use in the service businesses that you sold?"

"I used a long-term incentive plan designed to reward my managers' performance and their loyalty to the company."

"How did that work?" Alex asked.

"I gave managers targets and a corresponding bonus for achieving their personal targets. I paid them their bonus at the end of each year and put aside the exact same amount into a special pool of funds earmarked for them. Three years after launching the plan, and each year thereafter, they were allowed to withdraw one third of the pool. That way, their pool grew in value each year corresponding with their personal achievements but they could not access the extra money until three years after earning it. If they ever decided to leave, they would be walking away from three years worth of bonuses sitting in the pool."

"I thought acquiring companies wanted to see that management had real equity . . . "

"In my experience, an acquiring company wants to see that there is a management layer in place and that the management team has some form of long-term incentive plan that will encourage them to stay after the business is purchased. One way to do that is with equity, but equity and stock options are complicated to set up and may cause you all sorts of headaches down the road. If I look at it from Angie, Rhina, and Chris' collective point of view, a long-term incentive plan like the one I used in my businesses has a lot of benefits over equity. In a small service business, equity is only worth anything if there is a market for the shares. Assuming The Stapleton Agency will never go public—and I think that is a safe bet—then you may decide not to sell and then their shares are not worth much. As an employee, I'd much rather have an understandable cash bonus plan over being a minority shareholder in a closely held small business."

As they wrapped up the meeting, Ted asked Alex to spend the next week considering how he wanted to structure the compensation of his management team.

<table>
<tr><td>TED'S TIP #14</td><td>Only use equity as a last resort for motivating and retaining your management team. Consider alternative forms of long-term incentive plans.</td></tr>
</table>

Alex promoted Angie to vice president of sales, Rhina to vice president of client services, and Chris to vice president and creative director. His new management team was thrilled with their new titles. He gave them each a 7-percent pay raise and introduced a long-term incentive plan similar in design to the one Ted had described at their last meeting. Alex explained to his new management team that they were still a small business, they would each need to continue to do their jobs as before, and their promotion was designed to recognize them for the extra management tasks they were being asked to take on.

Alex left the office on Friday with a sense of satisfaction. He'd created and focused on a standard process that others could deliver, built a sales engine that produced excess cash, and established a management team with a long-term incentive plan.

He was close to having a sellable business.

9

Gaining Momentum

The next few months at The Stapleton Agency progressed according to Alex's plan. The new salespeople thrived under Angie's leadership. Rhina's attention to detail and inclination for creating process made her an excellent manager. Chris hired a third designer and continued to improve the efficiency of the Five-Step Logo Design Process. According to Harry, the financial results for the first six months of the year were equally impressive:

Revenue:	$1,280,000
Expenses:	$ 995,000
Pre-Tax Profit:	$ 285,000

At the halfway point of the year, Alex was tracking to exceed both his revenue targets and his profit margin goal.

****

Mary Pradham asked to meet Alex over lunch, which was strange. He'd not heard from Mary for six months; his accounts were in good standing; and Alex usually met Mary at her office at the downtown branch of First National Bank, and not over lunch at one of the city's best restaurants.

The waiter arrived and Mary ordered sparkling water for the table. They worked through a painful few minutes of small talk. Mary had never asked Alex about his personal life so didn't have much of a foundation to work from. She resorted to weather and sports. She was stretching, and it showed.

After their lunch arrived and the waiter left, Alex brought the conversation back to business.

"It's been a while since we spoke last. Why did you want to have lunch?"

"I like to meet with all of my clients face to face a few times a year," Mary exaggerated. "It's been a while since I've seen you and, judging by your account activity, you guys have been busy."

Alex decided to put Mary out of her misery early and took her question as a springboard to describe their new focus on logos, charging up front, the sales engine, and the building of his team.

"That's great, Alex. I think I have some other clients who could benefit from your focus."

Lunch plates were cleared and coffee arrived. Mary got down to business.

"I think I can get you a better rate of return on the money you have on deposit with us."

Alex nodded and gestured for Mary to continue.

She looked around to see if anyone was in earshot, lowering her voice as she spoke.

"As of this morning, you have $230,000 in your account and, judging by the pattern of your deposits, you're not going to need that money in the foreseeable future. Have you ever thought about high yield CDs?"

Alex listened politely as Mary droned on about FDIC insurance and interest rates.

After an exhaustive summary of the many features of First National Bank's deposit products, Mary launched into her next pitch. "If you ever want to expand, we'd be there to support you."

"What exactly do you mean by 'support you'?" Alex asked, tiring of Mary's duplicity.

"We have very good rates on credit lines. You have a $150,000 line of credit now but I'm sure I could get the credit group to up that to $300,000, maybe more . . . "

Alex couldn't believe his ears. In the space of six months, Mary had gone from hounding him like a loan shark to offering a credit line increase over lunch at one of the better restaurants in town. The irony was breathtaking. Alex thought about calling Mary on her change of tune but instead just smiled, sat back, and relished being courted by First National Bank.

****

The second half of the year progressed well. Angie's team was consistently selling one logo per week. Rhina had taken the instruction manual for the Five-Step Logo Design Process to an entirely new level of detail that Alex was convinced would rival a lunar landing briefing. Chris was busy and enjoyed mentoring his growing team of young designers. With five weeks left to go, Harry projected the year would end as follows:

Revenue:	$2,715,000
Expenses:	$2,225,000
Pre-Tax Profit:	$ 490,000

Alex was looking forward to spending a day planning his next year.

****

Pros & Cons

It rained all day at the beach house. Alex marveled at the power of the ocean and the beauty of watching the storm from Ted's retreat. Given the weather, Alex spent an uninterrupted day planning.

The past year had been full of milestones: Angie and her team had more than doubled sales. Chris' designers had created more than 250 logos and, judging by the number of clients who were coming back to see Rhina for new product and division launches, she had cultivated a happy group of repeat customers.

Alex had built a foundation on which he could grow. He decided to set his annual target at $5 million in revenue with a 20 percent pre-tax profit margin. That night, Alex drafted an email to update Ted on his progress:

> *Ted:*
>
> *Thanks for letting me use your beach house for my annual planning again this year. I'm going to shoot for $5,000,000 in revenue and $1,000,000 in pre-tax profit! I'll give you the details when I see you on Tuesday.*
>
> *Alex*

****

Alex started their Tuesday meeting with a quick update of the numbers. Ted listened and smiled at Alex's progress. He got up from his chair and walked over to the window, then turned to face Alex.

"When we first started our work together, The Stapleton Agency was a miserable business to own. Your team was being asked to do work they were not qualified to do; you were doing all of the sales and account management; your cash flow was tight; and you hadn't had a vacation in a while."

Alex cast his mind back to life 18 months ago.

"Yes, it seems like a long time ago. I'm having a lot more fun now."

"I thought you might be, which is why I want to revisit your decision to sell your company. If this year goes as planned, you're on track to generate $1 million in pre-tax profit. Your business is not as stressful as it used to be. You're not in a capital intensive business and, with your positive cash flow cycle, you could probably declare a big bonus this year and keep growing the company as you have been doing."

Alex sat silently absorbing Ted comments. He'd been on a one-track journey to sell the business for more than a year and hadn't indulged himself in thoughts of a different strategy.

Ted asked Alex to join him at his desk so that they could both look at his computer monitor. Ted had created a spreadsheet with two columns on it. The first column was labeled with the date one year from today. The second column was dated six years from today. Ted had plugged in some numbers in rows labeled Revenue, EBITDA, and Multiple.

"What's with the spreadsheet?"

"Alex, if you achieve a pre-tax bottom line of $1 million this year, you may be able to sell your business for $5 million, which was the goal you had when we met one year ago."

With this declaration, Ted pointed to a field on his spreadsheet labeled Sale Proceeds and the number $5,000,000 filled the cell. Alex couldn't help but crack a smile at the thought.

"However, you could choose to keep your business. You would need to shoulder all of the risk and there would be tough patches. But if you kept the business for five more years and grew it at 20 percent per year—which is conservative given the pace you have been growing recently—your business could be worth $12 million or more."

Ted pointed to the spreadsheet.

"Selling your business is a big decision. The process will be stressful and will take a toll on you and your family. Once you sell, there is no going back. I'd like you to spend the week thinking about whether you've made the right decision. When you come back next week, if you still want to sell your company, we'll get started with the final steps in the process."

****

Alex needed to think and had to be away from the office. He found a Starbucks near Ted's office, ordered a Grande Bold, and sat in a quiet corner. He opened his notebook to an empty page and did what his mother had always taught him to do when he faced a big decision: he drew a line vertically down the center of the page and wrote the word *Pros* on the left and *Cons* on the right. He started to scribble.

> ### Selling now
>
> | Pros | Cons |
> |---|---|
> | Time to travel with Pam | Give up the possibility of a larger payout |
> | Time with Jenny & Max | |
> | Pay off mortgage | |
> | Financial freedom | |
> | Less stress | |

Alex looked at the list and kept recalling the numbers Ted had calculated in their meeting. Five million dollars symbolized financial freedom. A financial planner had once told him that he could live on 4 percent of his investments in perpetuity. That meant that, after he paid tax on the sale of his business, he'd still have enough to draw a six-figure income each year from his nest egg for the rest of his life and never have to touch the principal. Jenny and Max would not be able to attend private school but they'd have their Dad around and Pam would be happy that the bank would take the guarantee off their home and their financial affairs would finally be secure.

Then Alex contemplated $12 million. With that much money, he'd have more than enough money to pay off his mortgage and travel. Then his imagination failed him. Alex could not think of any toys that were worth the risk. The marginal value of the extra $7 million was limited and the risks were considerable. If he kept the business another five years, the economy could turn, or a competitor could decide to specialize in logos. Angie could set up a competitive shop, he could be sued . . . Alex let his mind get carried away with doomsday scenarios.

He would rather have $5 million today than a chance for $12 million in five years. Perhaps that made him weak. Maybe Ted would think he was not a real businessman. It didn't matter—he'd made his decision to sell.

The Broker

Ted joined Alex on the chairs they had used every Tuesday morning for the last 18 months.

"Ted, thanks for creating the spreadsheet and forcing me to rethink my motivations for selling."

"You're welcome. It's a big decision."

"It is and I feel more confident than ever with my decision to sell my firm. At the end of the day, I'm a simple guy. I don't need a vacation home in Aspen or a private plane. I want to experience true financial freedom and $5 million would be enough."

"I'm glad you thought it through again and I'm happy to help you through the process. I want you to prepare yourself for a tough road. These last few steps will likely take six to eight months and it will be a bit of a roller coaster."

"I'm ready, Ted."

"Good. I think we're at a point where we need to start interviewing an advisor to represent you."

"You mean like an agent? Are you sure I need one?"

"A good broker will get you competitive offers and hopefully ask a lot of the tough questions behind the scenes."

"What kind of broker do you recommend?"

"Brokers come in all shapes and sizes. The ideal is to find a broker for whom you will be a meaningful account. The term *business broker* is usually used for individuals who do smaller deals where the total value of the transaction is well under $5 million. You're really looking for a boutique mergers & acquisitions firm. The firm you select needs to be large enough to be respected by a potential buyer, yet small enough that your deal will be important to them. Ideally they will have also done some deals in your industry."

"Do you know anyone I could speak to?" Alex asked.

"I'd recommend you speak with Mark Travers. He's with Travers Capital Partners; Cindy can give you his number. Also speak with Peggy Moyles. Peggy is a partner with EMG Capital Partners."

TED'S TIP #15 | *Find an advisor for whom you will be neither their largest nor their smallest client. Make sure they know your industry.*

****

The office of Travers Capital Partners was downtown. The receptionist looked bemused as Alex approached. She greeted him coolly and assured Alex that Mr. Travers would be down to greet him shortly. After 10 minutes, a woman walked through a set of doors and introduced herself as Amanda, Mark Travers' assistant. She instructed Alex to follow her up a spiral staircase that connected the two floors of Travers Capital Partners.

Amanda ushered Alex into a boardroom looking out over the city. Alex counted 12 Aeron chairs situated around a large glass boardroom table. He felt a little self-conscious sitting at such an obviously oversized table, so he situated himself on one end near the door. Amanda returned and produced a large bottle of Perrier. There was a tall glass with ice and three neatly cut limes on the edge of a silver serving plate. Alex passed the time looking at a muted flat screen television with CNBC rolling through stock quotes as if the capital markets were some sort of spectator sport. Finally, Mark Travers appeared, offering a firm handshake and a toothy smile.

"So, Alex, how do you know Ted Gordon?"

"He's an old family friend. How did you meet Ted?"

"We represented the buyer of Ted's consulting business. He's a smart guy and a tough negotiator. Tell me a little bit about your agency."

"We're not really an agency anymore. We specialize in producing logos. We do a lot of logos for companies launching new divisions or new products."

"Interesting. We know a lot of the marketing agencies in town. Who's your creative director?"

"His name is Chris Sawchuk and I doubt you know him. We don't consider ourselves a marketing agency per se. Our Five-Step Logo Design Process is all we do. We've become very efficient at creating logos."

Mark started to wave his hands, which Alex took to mean he had received some sort of flash of brilliance from above. Alex stopped to let Mark say whatever had gotten him so animated.

"I know the perfect company to buy your business," Mark declared.

Alex was surprised to hear that Mark already had an idea of who would buy The Stapleton Agency after just a few minutes of discussion. Intrigued, he asked Mark to elaborate.

"Look, we do a lot of work for Multicom."

Alex recognized Multicom as the largest agency holding company in the world with more than $1 billion in annual revenue and operations around the world.

"The Stapleton Agency is just the kind of tuck-in acquisition Multicom would love. I'd be happy to arrange a meeting with their North American business development executive."

"Sounds great, Mark. How do you guys work with your clients?"

Mark went on to explain that they charged 5 percent of the deal but typically worked with much larger companies. He said under normal circumstances he would not take on a firm as small as The Stapleton Agency but since Ted referred Alex and he already had a good relationship with Multicom, he'd represent Alex as a favor to Ted.

Alex left Travers Capital Partners with mixed feelings. On one hand, he thought Mark was successful and certainly well-connected to Multicom. On the other hand, something didn't seem quite right. It all sounded a little too easy.

****

Alex's next meeting was with Peggy Moyles at EMG Capital Partners. She greeted Alex and ushered him into her office. Peggy asked him to describe his business and Alex proceeded to outline the work they had done to remake The Stapleton Agency into a company with a single offering.

"Alex, you've done something most service business owners never do, which is to extract yourself from the epicenter of your operations. You have a predictable sales engine with a good pipeline of recurring revenue. Your positive cash flow will be attractive to buyers, your capital structure is simple, and the management team seems to be engaged for the long term. You've built an excellent business."

"Thanks, Peggy. I had an exploratory meeting yesterday with Mark Travers over at Travers Capital Partners and he thought we would be a good fit for Multicom. What are your thoughts on Multicom as a potential buyer?"

"They would not have been my first choice. Big agencies have a standard formula by which they buy companies and it typically involves a 3 – 5-year earn out. In addition, big agencies think all companies want to be like them. I don't think they would value or appreciate all the work you've done to specialize in a single process."

Alex was impressed with Peggy's appreciation of the work he had done to move away from the agency model. He pressed Peggy for some names of possible buyers.

"I'd like to have the opportunity to think about it some more, but off the top of my head, I could see one of the technology firms with a big investment in color printing hardware or maybe a large printing company might be interested. You could act as a Trojan horse for a company that wants the printing contracts of the companies you create logos for."

Alex liked the way Peggy was thinking.

She went on to describe how her firm worked. They charged 5 percent of the deal but also wanted a retainer of $7,000 per month over the next six months. Alex asked Peggy if she would waive the retainer and her response was crisp.

"We need to charge a retainer to ensure that you're serious about selling your business. If we took on assignments without a retainer, we'd spin our wheels generating offers for owners who were not serious about selling their firms."

Alex understood Peggy's position, but wondered why Mark Travers wasn't charging a retainer.

****

Alex started their Tuesday meeting with a description of the meetings with Mark Travers and Peggy Moyles.

"So who are you going to go with?" Ted asked

"I'm not sure. I like that Mark knows the Multicom guys. He seemed to think it would be possible to get an offer from Multicom in the next few weeks."

"I understand, Alex, but if you want my advice, I'd avoid using Mark. It sounds like he wants to deliver a gift to Multicom in an effort to ingratiate his firm. Mark makes a lot of his money from representing buyers, and Multicom is a big client of Travers Capital Partners. It sounds like he would try to deliver you to Multicom without creating any competitive tension. Without that competition, you might be disappointed by Multicom's offer and you would have wasted a lot of time."

"I never considered that, but is there anything wrong with going with Mark to see if he can get a good offer from Multicom? Since he's not charging a retainer, I don't see what I have to lose."

"Once you engage an M&A firm, the chances others will find out you are interested in selling will go up. Mark will agree to keep things confidential but the more people know of your intentions, the higher the chances are it will get back to your staff or customers."

Alex pondered Ted's warning for a moment and switched gears.

"Peggy wants a retainer."

"That's not necessarily a bad thing. She's going to act for you exclusively and she will still be motivated because most of her compensation will come from getting you a deal. She's a professional and needs some way of making sure you're serious. Plus, Peggy appreciates the fact that you're not just another marketing agency."

"You have a lot more experience with using M&A firms so I'm inclined to choose Peggy based on what you're saying."

"I think she'll serve you well."

TED'S TIP #16	*Avoid an advisor who offers to broker a discussion with a single client. You want to ensure there is competition for your business and avoid being used as a pawn for your advisor to curry favor with his or her best client.*

10

A Blank Check for Growth

Once hired, Peggy asked Alex to provide a three-year business plan for The Stapleton Agency. She wanted Alex to include financial projections along with a description of the target market and the overall opportunity Alex envisioned for the business of creating logos. Peggy explained that Alex's plan would become the foundation for a lot of her work and it was important for the plan to be solid.

Alex had never planned more than one year in advance and found the process of writing a three-year plan daunting. One assumption led to the next and, by year three of the plan, Alex felt like he was writing a work of fiction. In writing the financial projections, Alex anticipated a 20 percent top-line growth rate for the next three years. He kept his 20-percent profit margin goal steady. Once complete, Alex emailed the plan to Ted to get his input.

****

Ted asked Alex to meet him at Starbucks across the street from his office.

"Good morning, Alex," Ted said, smiling. "What are you having?"

Ted turned to the Barista and ordered a Grande Bold and a bottle of water. They found a quiet table in the corner and Alex began.

"What do you think of the plan?"

"It's a good start. Before we get into the plan, I want to talk coffee."

Alex was puzzled. "I noticed you ordered water. We didn't have to meet here for my benefit. You know we could have . . . "

"No. I wanted to meet here to talk about Starbucks. They've built an amazing business, don't you think?"

Alex didn't know where Ted was going with this but continued to play along.

"They have stores on just about every street corner in America."

"And they're all pretty much the same. They even have their own language that you coffee drinkers have all learned fluently."

"What does this have to do with my plan?"

"Alex, I'm challenging you to sprinkle a little Starbucks in your plan."

"What do you mean?"

"When a company looks for an acquisition, it's usually because they want to grow. Often, they are not able to grow as fast as they want organically so they acquire companies to bolster their top line revenue. For you to get the highest valuation for The Stapleton Agency, you need to show how you can be an engine of growth for an acquirer."

"What does that have to do with Starbucks?" Alex asked.

"When you write your next draft, think about how aggressively Starbucks has grown. Imagine that you have a blank check to grow The Stapleton Agency as large and as fast as you possibly could given unlimited resources. You need to paint the picture for an acquirer of what is possible for the business of creating logos."

"But isn't that like lying?"

"Not at all. Your plan has to be possible but not necessarily achievable on your own. Peggy is going to approach companies that are a lot larger than you. They will have more money, more physical offices, more employees, more of everything. If you can plug The Stapleton Agency into a big company's resources, you will be able to grow much more quickly than you could on your own."

"How do I write the plan without knowing who the acquirer will be and exactly what resources they have?"

"The best way to do it at this point is to imagine you have a blank check and unlimited resources. There will be plenty of time for an acquiring company to scrutinize your plan and discount your projections based on what they think is reasonable. I want you to take off your conservative business owner hat and imagine what is possible. Could you start a satellite office in every major city in the country? Could you double your sales force? Could you make better use of the Internet to sell logos? Think like Starbucks."

Ted wished Alex luck and left. Alex ordered a refill and started scribbling notes.

TED'S TIP #17	*Write a three-year business plan that paints a picture of what is possible for your business. Think big; remember that the company that acquires you will have more resources for you to accelerate your growth.*

****

Draft two of the plan was more fun to write. Alex suspended reality and imagined satellite sales offices of The Stapleton Agency in five cities around the U.S. He planned a telephone operation with eight phone reps selling the Five-Step Logo Design Process to small businesses in rural America with no access to design resources. The new plan called for revenue of $12 million in three years. The more Alex wrote, the more he believed the plan was actually possible if he found the right acquirer.

Alex emailed draft two of the plan to Ted.

****

Ted's response came over email a few hours later:

Alex:

I like the new plan. Lots of Starbucks—I think it will serve you well.

I'd recommend you make one small change: stop referring to this year's financials as a "forecast." You need to communicate that you're confident in this year's projections. Instead, refer to your projections for this year as "Current Year." By the time we get to the offer stage, you will be three quarters of the way through this year and you want an acquiring company basing their offer on $5 million in revenue and $1 million in profit, not last year's numbers. It's a subtle shift but it's important.

Great job!

Ted

Alex walked over to the whiteboard in the middle of the office. He saw that his salespeople were tracking well to plan. Each sales rep had at least six appointments set for the week and they were each on target to sell four logos for the month.

He walked back to his office and opened draft two of the plan on his desktop. He found the page that referred to his financial goals for this year and replaced the word "Forecast" with "Current Year."

The Teaser

Peggy Moyles was in her late forties. Salads for lunch and a daily appointment with a treadmill ensured that she looked five years younger. She had just come from a lunchtime Pilates class designed to help her posture, which, on the occasion of her first working session with Alex, was good. She offered Alex a firm handshake as he arrived at the offices of EMG Capital Partners.

She took Alex to a small boardroom where she arranged two copies of the plan Alex had emailed her, pencils, a calculator, and two bottles of water.

"Alex, the purpose of today's meeting is for me to understand your plan in enough detail that I can write a two-page teaser about your business and start work on The Book."

Alex needed a primer on the language of a deal. "What's a teaser?"

"A teaser is a one- or two-page description of your business, which announces that your company is for sale and paints the picture of the opportunity your business offers a potential buyer."

"But won't my employees and customers find out that the company is for sale?"

"No. We disguise the teaser so that your business is anonymous. If an acquiring company is interested, we'll send them a Non-Disclosure Agreement. If they sign the NDA, then we'll send them a complete description of your business and your plan. We call that The Book."

"How many people will you send the teaser to?"

"Ideally, we should agree to a shortlist of around 20 companies. I've started a long list and I'd like your help to narrow it down to just the companies with a compelling strategic reason to acquire The Stapleton Agency."

"I've heard about strategic buyers and financial buyers. I assume you're recommending we look for a strategic buyer."

"Strategic buyers will typically pay more because you're worth more to them than you would be worth to a financial buyer. A strategic buyer will model how you would perform as a business if they owned you and applied all of their resources to your business. A financial buyer is simply looking for a return on their investment and wouldn't bring much more that their checkbook to a deal. With few synergies to exploit, financial buyers will typically offer you a lower price to ensure they get a good return on their money."

"So which companies do you think would have a strategic reason to buy us?" Alex asked.

Peggy pulled out her long list of potential buyers and showed it to Alex.

"As you review it, consider the companies that have approached you for a partnership. Think about your suppliers and other companies you come into contact with. Your plan calls for more offices and more salespeople so think about companies who already have a lot of salespeople or offices in other cities. Which companies have the most synergies to exploit?"

Peggy and Alex brainstormed companies and rated each one for their strategic fit. After two hours, Peggy narrowed the list to 23 companies with a compelling strategic reason to acquire The Stapleton Agency. Each company had enough cash to buy Alex's company and, as far as Peggy was aware, was open to the idea of an acquisition.

Optics

For the first time that spring, Alex opened the sunroof. It was the last Tuesday in March and the sun showed the first signs of warmth after a long winter.

Alex started their Tuesday get-together with a description of his meeting with Peggy. Ted waved him off.

"Before we talk about Peggy, give me this week's numbers."

Alex was caught off guard as he had expected Ted to want to spend their Tuesday time on Peggy's work. Nevertheless, he thought back to the whiteboard and summarized their progress.

"We're on track. Angie's team sold eight logos last week, which makes 27 for the month and we still have three selling days left in the month. Rhina just hired another account director so she now has five people on her team. Chris is interviewing another designer next week and our old client Natural Foods has come back again for another logo. This time Ziggy is launching a line of organic chocolate milk."

"I thought tree huggers were all about healthy living," Ted said with a cheeky grin.

Having dispensed with the banter, Ted got serious.

"Alex, your work with Peggy is going to eat up a lot of your time. As hard as it is going to be, you have to keep your eyes on The Stapleton Agency's performance. You have to make sure your current year projections are achieved."

"I'll keep my eye on the ball," Alex said.

"There's one other thing I want you to think about. I noticed you used the word 'client' to describe Natural Foods."

"Yes. Ziggy's been a client of ours for a while."

"That's good, but I want you to replace the word 'client' with the word 'customer' when you talk about the companies that buy your process."

Alex couldn't believe Ted was nitpicking over a single word.

"Why does that matter?"

"Service firms refer to their customers as clients and product businesses refer to them as customers. You've worked hard to transform The Stapleton Agency from a service business into a product business with a standard scalable and repeatable process. Using words like client subtly communicates to a potential buyer that you still think of yourself as a service business."

"It's just a word. Surely that can't matter to a potential buyer," Alex said.

"At this point in the process, optics matter a lot. An acquiring company will be trying to put you in a box in their mind. They have a box for product companies and a corresponding process for acquiring them. They have a different box in their mind for acquiring service businesses and you don't want to land in that box."

"Why not?"

"Because their service business box has a formula for acquiring a businesses that uses a 3 – 5-year earn out with only a small amount of cash up front. If you land in their service business box, you'll get an offer with most of your money at risk and tied to an earn out. You take all of the risk and they get most of the reward. You're going to have to agree to leave some of your money in an earn out but our goal is to get you as much cash up front as you can. That means doing whatever you can to communicate the fact that The Stapleton Agency is not a plain old service business."

TED'S TIP #18

Stop using the language of a service firm and start using the language of a sellable business. Change words like clients to customers and firm to business. Rid your website and customer-facing communications of any references that reveal you used to be a generic service business.

"So I need to start referring to clients as customers."

"Yes. And think about the other words you use that are the typical lingo of a service business. I'd change the word 'firm' and refer to The Stapleton Agency as a 'company' instead. Replace the word 'engagement' with the word 'contract'. You want to do whatever you can to communicate to a buyer that you're a real business, not just a flighty collection of temperamental professional service providers."

11

Telling Management

It was well after 5:00 p.m. and The Stapleton Agency was still a hive of activity. Alex felt like an unfaithful spouse returning from an encounter with a lover as he mingled with his staff.

"Hey, Angie, how was your day?"

"The team's doing well. We've closed two deals and have scheduled nine new appointments this afternoon. The guys are staying late because I promised them drinks were on me if they could schedule 20 appointments in a single afternoon."

Smiling at how much Angie enjoyed motivating her flock, Alex sauntered over to Rhina's office, expecting her to be gone for the day. Rhina was still in the office and meeting with one of her account directors on the Natural Foods chocolate milk assignment.

Rhina saw Alex approaching and waved him over.

"We found out today that if Natural Foods were a famous Hollywood star, they would be Sarah Jessica Parker," Rhina said with a smile.

"How is my friend Ziggy doing?" Alex asked.

"She's great and says hi."

Alex continued his tour and saw Chris at his desk proofing one of the logos that was about to go to stage five of the process. Alex was less surprised to see Chris at his desk because he had been working late for the past four days.

"Don't sleep here tonight," Alex said jokingly.

"I won't. We're just about finished for the day," Chris said optimistically.

Alex felt a pang of guilt as he walked back to his office. His staff was working well after 5:00 p.m. while Alex had spent the day contemplating the sale of his business. Alex knew he would be the only one to gain financially from the sale of The Stapleton Agency and somehow that didn't seem right.

****

It was unusually cold for the first week in April and Alex stuffed his hands into the pockets of his raincoat as he jogged from his car to the offices of EMG Capital Partners. Alex was meeting with Peggy at her office to discuss the teaser distribution.

She began with a summary of their progress to date: all 23 companies short-listed had been contacted. Seven companies had declined, saying they were working on other deals, while four companies had requested The Book and agreed to sign the NDA. Peggy was waiting to hear back from the remaining 12 companies.

"Great progress," Alex said.

"Yes, we're happy with the reaction to the teaser so far. It's still in the early days, but so far so good."

"What's the next step in the process once The Book has been distributed?"

"We need to schedule management presentations with the interested parties."

"I'll need to meet with these people in person?"

"Yes."

Peggy sat quietly considering if it was the right time to raise a delicate issue. Her rapport with Alex had been good so far so she decided to proceed.

"Alex, as part of the management presentations, we'll need to involve your management team. It's important for a potential buyer to see the next layer of management who will be responsible for the business if and when you leave."

"If I tell them I'm thinking of selling, I have no idea how they'll react. I mean they helped me to build our business. They put their heart and soul into our success. There's no telling how they'll react when I tell them I'm selling out."

"You'll need to tell them sooner or later. And I'd recommend sooner. Even if I can convince a prospective buyer to meet with you on your own for the management presentation, eventually they will want to meet your team. Plus, as more people get The Book, despite the NDA, the higher the odds are that one of your team will find out. I'm sure you'd rather tell them directly than have them find out some other way."

Alex left Peggy's office wondering how to tell Angie, Rhina, and Chris that the guy they had placed their faith in, and worked so hard for, was about to sell out to the highest possible bidder.

****

Ted was immersed in something at his desk as Alex arrived. Alex shared the week's sales numbers and gave Ted an update on his progress with Peggy.

Sensing there was something else on Alex's mind, Ted asked, "Alex, you seem a little introspective today. What are you thinking about?"

"Peggy thinks we're going to have three or four companies interested in making an offer and the next stage in the process involves management presentations."

"That's great news."

"I guess so, but Peggy thinks each of the bidders will need to meet with Angie, Rhina, and Chris so I'll have to tell them I'm thinking of selling the business."

"That's a delicate conversation. What are your biggest concerns?"

"I feel guilty. I think they're going to look at me and resent the fact that I'm cashing in."

"Alex, I understand the way you're feeling. I felt the same way when I sold my first business."

"And how did your employees take it?"

"At first they were a little surprised but after they had time to process the news, they started to warm to the idea."

"They actually liked the idea?"

"Yes. Working for a small business can have advantages but the possibilities for career advancement are limited. They look at the highest rung of the ladder every time you walk into the office and know that as long as you own the business, their advancement is going to be limited."

"I get that they might see career opportunities, but it's hard to integrate two companies and there are always redundancies . . ."

"Merging two companies can be a challenge. However, there are also a lot of opportunities that emerge when a big company swallows a small one. Ambitious people want to paint on a bigger canvass. Big companies have big budgets and important projects, and operate on a level of professionalism that your best people will enjoy. If they play it right, Angie, Rhina, and Chris could benefit from some career mobility if you are acquired."

"They may see opportunities, but aren't they going to be jealous that I walk away with a check and all they get is a new boss?"

"Alex, you've worked hard to build The Stapleton Agency. You took all of the risk and, for better or worse, capitalism rewards risk taking. It was you who trudged up to First National Bank every other day groveling for work. You were the one who lost sleep every time Mary Pradham called. It was your home the bank would have taken had you defaulted on your operating line."

"But I'd still like to find a way to let them benefit financially if we are acquired."

"Fair enough. Keep in mind they will each benefit personally if a strategic buyer acquires you because the acquirer will come with strategic assets—like offices in other cities and investment dollars—that will make it easier for Angie, Rhina, and Chris to reach their personal objectives and corresponding bonuses. They also have a long-term incentive plan that will pay out at higher levels corresponding with their higher bonuses."

"Maybe I should throw in some stock options as well to sweeten the deal for my team. They've been with me for a while."

"Your intentions are admirable but misguided. Stock options will further complicate the process of selling your business.

113

You'll have to draft a shareholders agreement. Minority shareholders have rights. You will be morally, and to some extent legally, required to keep Angie, Rhina, and Chris in the loop as you review offers. Selling your business is hard enough. You don't need three other opinions at the table. My advice would be to keep it clean and give your management team a simple, one-time cash bonus if you successfully sell your business as a thank you for helping you with the management meetings and their dedication to the business. That way you're giving them a cash incentive to participate in the management meetings and sharing in your rewards. But I wouldn't get carried away. They're already benefiting from the chance of career advancement and a higher probability of achieving their personal bonus targets and corresponding long-term incentive plan."

Alex left Ted's office feeling better about the prospects of telling his management team.

TED'S TIP #19	*Don't issue stock options to retain key employees after an acquisition. Instead, use a simple stay bonus that offers the members of your management team a cash reward if you sell your company. Pay the reward in two or more installments only to those who stay so that you ensure your key staff stays on through the transition.*

A meeting with Angie, Rhina, and Chris was arranged for the last Friday in April. Alex was not one for early morning meetings so his leadership team was already buzzing about the possible reasons for the meeting.

He greeted his team and was surprised at how nervous he felt. Alex had made important presentations to larger audiences full of people he didn't know. He was about to present to just three people he'd known and worked with for more than a year yet he was noticeably nervous.

"Thanks for coming in early for this session. I wanted to start early to ensure we don't get interrupted by the rest of the team. I've been spending a lot of time out of the office over the last few months to plan the next stage of our growth as a company. I think you guys have proven that we have a scalable model for creating logos. We've done well here in town and I think we can do even more if we start to expand geographically."

The team sat up in their seats, proud to be working for a successful, growing company and excited about the prospect of new locations and growing the business.

"It's become clear to me that for us to get to the next level, we're going to need a partner. A company with deep pockets and a broad geographic footprint."

Alex let his last comment settle in before proceeding.

Angie spoke first. "So you're selling the business?"

"I'm exploring the idea, yes."

Alex went on to position the sale in the context of what it would mean for Angie, Rhina, and Chris. He explained that, with the right acquirer, there would be the possibility of career advancements for each of them and that their personal objectives should become easier to meet. He also promised them each a $10,000 bonus as a thank you if the company was sold.

The team was silent for a moment.

"Alex, I think this is a great step for you. I think we've all known for a while that you were planning to sell," said Chris.

"You did?"

"For sure," said Rhina. "You're an entrepreneur. You like the startup and the variety. But we're beyond that stage now and frankly we don't need you as much anymore. Like Chris, I'm really happy for you and will do what I can to help."

"I don't think it will come as a surprise to anyone in this room that I'm ambitious," said Angie. "I would enjoy building an even bigger team and operating on a bigger playing field. I agree with Chris and Rhina, I'm happy for you and I think you're making a good decision."

Alex was stunned.

He couldn't believe how much he'd been dreading telling his management team. He felt indebted to each of them for how positively they had reacted to the news. That night, he drove home feeling 10 pounds lighter.

12

The Question

Babylon had been rated as one of the city's finest restaurants for three years running. Alex was ushered to a small private room where his hosts were waiting. Peggy Moyles sat at a large round table flanked by two overweight men. Alex estimated they were in their late forties, although years of hard living may have inflated his estimate. He greeted Peggy and she introduced him to Alistair McGrath and Simon Tupper.

Alistair was the president of RTX Printing, which was the largest division of RTX Global, a billion dollar U.K.-based conglomerate that owned everything from radio stations to trade shows. RTX Printing was the second largest offset printer in the U.S. and Alistair knew that becoming the largest was his ticket back to London. Simon was McGrath's head of business development.

Peggy had known Alistair for a decade, having sold him a number of small printing companies over the years. She had approached him about The Stapleton Agency opportunity and had suggested a management presentation at RTX's U.S. headquarters but Alistair suggested dinner as a first step instead.

"A pleasure to meet you," Alistair said to Alex, revealing his strong English accent.

"Likewise," Alex responded, offering both Alistair and Simon a firm handshake.

"You're working with a true professional with Ms. Moyles," Alistair said as he gestured to Peggy. "How did you two meet?"

"A friend of mine referred Peggy."

Small talk continued. A waiter arrived and offered the group a menu and Alistair the cocktail he was craving. Alistair started with Scotch and Simon ordered a Grey Goose and tonic, while Peggy and Alex ordered sparkling water for the table.

Drinks arrived, and the group ordered their meal. With the waiter out of the room for an extended period, Alex launched into a series of questions he had prepared for RTX. He wanted to understand RTX's ambitions for the U.S. market and how they planned to diversify further. He pretended to be interested in the culture they had built and RTX's global presence.

Alistair, more interested in the wine list, deferred to Simon to answer Alex's queries on behalf of RTX. The sommelier noticed Alistair studying the wine list and offered his services.

"I understand three of you ordered the tenderloin this evening. I suggest the 2001 White Hall Lane Cabernet. It was a great year in Napa."

"That sounds fine," Alistair said.

Alex wondered just how much a good year in Napa would cost the shareholders of RTX Global.

"Tell me a little bit about The Stapleton Agency," asked Simon.

Alex went on to describe the Five-Step Logo Design Process and his sales team as Simon and Alistair listened. Peggy stayed largely silent, letting Alex handle the questions. Steaks arrived and RTX's shareholders were stung for another bottle of White Hall Lane. Alistair concentrated on his steak, content to let Simon and Alex carry the conversation.

Plates were cleared and coffee ordered. As the waiter left the room, Alistair adjusted his chair slightly to square himself to Alex. They made eye contact and Alistair asked the only real question of the evening.

"So Alex, tell me something. Why do you want to sell your business?"

The question was so simple and obvious that Alex kicked himself for not rehearsing an answer. He had anticipated questions about his sales process, his cash flow, and profit margin but this one simple question had him on the defensive. His heart raced and he could feel his face become flushed. He kicked himself for drinking the second glass of wine. Buying some time, he raised his napkin to his lips and pretended there was some sort of offensive debris left over from dinner. Finally, he answered truthfully.

"It's been almost 10 years since I started The Stapleton Agency. We've had a good run but I'm ready to spend more time with my kids and do some traveling with my wife."

Alistair seemed satisfied with the response and turned the conversation to sports. Alex sat back and polished off the last mouthful of wine in his glass.

****

They said their goodbyes on the sidewalk outside of Babylon. Alistair and Simon congratulated Alex on the success of his business and promised to get back to Peggy next week.

It was an unusually warm night for May so they walked slowly. Alex offered to escort Peggy back to her car parked a couple of blocks away.

"That seemed to go well. What do you think?" asked Alex.

"I think they're going to pass."

"What do you mean? They just said they'd be in touch next week."

"They're not interested."

"How do you know?"

"Look, I've been doing this long enough to know that dinner was just window dressing. The only question that mattered was when Alistair asked you why you want to sell your business. Once he heard your answer, the meeting was over as far as he was concerned."

Alex's mind went back to replay his answer.

"Peggy, I responded truthfully. Did you want me to lie?"

"No, I don't want you to lie but there is a right and a wrong way to answer that question. A buyer wants to hear that you see a future for your business and you want their help to get you to the next level. They want to hear you personally are going to stay on after the sale."

"But Peggy, I thought I was clear that I didn't want a deal with a 3–5 year earn out. I'm willing to stay on for a while, but I want to go do something else."

"I understand but there is a right way and a wrong way to say that."

"What do you suggest?"

"Tell them you're proud of the growth you've achieved and that you're at a point in your life where you'd like to create some liquidity for the value you've created so far *and* have an opportunity to participate in some of the future upside of the business."

"But that's not exactly true. I want to sell my business."

"I understand that, but my job is to get you the highest possible price with the largest possible percentage up front. To do that, a buyer needs to feel motivated and to feel motivated they need to hear you're genuinely keen on tapping into their resources to help you get to the next level."

Peggy added, "Alex, buyers understand that entrepreneurs want to put some cash in their jeans but nobody wants to buy a sinking ship where the captain is about to jump. They need to feel like you see a future for the business and that you're excited about exploiting the assets they have. They need to feel like you're willing to stay on for a period of time to help them tap into some of the synergies of the two businesses."

"How long are you suggesting?"

"We don't have to pinpoint a time frame now, but you do need to give the buyer the sense that you're willing to stay on for a transition period. Leaving it vague would be best at this point. Once you have been acquired, you'll become an employee of the acquirer and, just like any employee, it will be up to them to find a way to keep you engaged. For me to get you the best deal possible, with the most cash up front, they need to hear the things I just mentioned."

Alex drove home disappointed. He'd blown a good opportunity with RTX and was embarrassed. He came off like a farm league rookie and the boys from RTX played big league ball.

The Options

Marcus Knightsbridge adjusted his glasses and used his fingers to comb the bangs away from his eyes. Alex thought Marcus looked somewhat disheveled to be the lead business development executive for Print Technology Group.

"Alex, can you please explain your sales cycle."

Alex, Peggy, and Marcus had been holed up in the boardroom of EMG Capital Partners for more than two hours. Print Technology Group, the third largest provider of color printers in the U.S., had responded to Peggy's teaser. Like RTX, Print Technology Group thought The Stapleton Agency could supply them with a steady flow of new business leads, all of whom would want to print their new logo on one of Print Technology Group's full color printers.

Marcus had been provided with The Book and, sufficiently impressed, requested a management presentation from The Stapleton Agency. Marcus continued to plod through his list of questions. By the fourth hour, Peggy proposed a break. It was a beautiful July day so Peggy took them to a French restaurant with a patio across the street from her office. Lunch was a welcome reprieve from Marcus' relentless questioning. They dined and enjoyed some relatively easy banter.

Peggy excused herself for a visit to the ladies room, leaving Marcus and Alex alone. Marcus brought the conversation around to business and the purpose of his trip.

"Alex, it seems like you've built a great business and it's growing nicely. Out of curiosity, why do you want to sell?"

This time, Alex was prepared.

"We've proven the model can work in one city. I'm at a stage of my life personally that I'd like to create some liquidity for the value I've created so far, and I'd like to find a partner who can help us replicate the model in other cities and allow me to share in some of the future growth."

Alex was proud of himself for getting it out of his mouth without stuttering or sounding too rehearsed. His only regret was that Peggy missed his performance.

****

Harry arrived at The Stapleton Agency on time. He wore a blue golf shirt tucked into a pleated pair of chinos. He had managed to hike his belt so high that his waistline appeared to rest just under his rib cage. He was at The Stapleton Agency for a midyear review.

"You guys are doing really well, Alex. Your revenue for the first six months of the year was more than $2.4 million. You've already put $450,000 on the bottom line and you're only six months into the year. At this rate, you may exceed $1 million in pre-tax profit this year. Given where you were a couple of years ago, that's an amazing achievement."

Alex smiled and knew he was on track to deliver the year-end projections he had provided Peggy.

****

It had been two weeks since the Print Technology Group management presentation with Marcus and Peggy was starting to get worried. There'd been no communication from Marcus, which seemed odd to Peggy, given how well the meeting had gone. Rather than wait for Print Technology Group, Peggy had devised a backup plan and asked Alex to join her at EMG Capital Partners for a meeting.

"Alex, I know we've been going down the road of finding you a strategic buyer like Print Technology Group but I had an interesting lunch last week with an acquaintance from Springboard Private Capital Partners. I told him about your business and he'd like to know more about The Stapleton Agency."

"Sounds intriguing . . . "

"We do a lot of work with Springboard so I know how they do deals. They like investing in growing companies like The Stapleton Agency."

"Are you talking about a private equity company?"

"Yes. If they like your business, they would buy half of your company, which allows you to put some money in your pocket. Then they invest more of their cash—probably about $1 million in your case—to help you get to the next level."

"What kind of valuation would they use?"

"Springboard bought a marketing service business last year and valued the company at 3 – 4 times pre-tax profit."

"Sounds a little low to me. And they'd only buy half of my business and want me to stay on for another five years?" Alex said in disbelief.

"Yes, they're not operators. They're financial buyers who would inject more money into your operations and would be looking for a significant return on their investment."

Alex didn't need much time to respond.

"Peggy, I'm surprised that you even consider this a possibility. You know we're a cash flow positive business. If we wanted to re-invest in the business, we'd have plenty of cash to do that now. The valuation is low and the idea of staying on for five years is a non-starter with me."

"Fair enough. My job is to bring you all of the options, that's all."

"I understand. Any word from Print Technology Group?"

"Nothing yet."

13

A Sellable Company

The call came in on Alex's mobile. It was 7:00 p.m. and the August sun was still warm enough for Alex to have the sunroof open. He closed the sunroof as he answered the call.

"Hey, Alex. It's Peggy."

"What's up?"

"Good news. I think Print Technology Group is preparing an offer."

A rush of adrenalin came over Alex and he had to pull over into a gas station.

"That's great news, Peggy. Do you have any idea what they're thinking?"

"No. Marcus is a professional and wouldn't tip his hand over the phone. He's asked for some more background material on our three-year projections, which I need to get to him tomorrow. He told me he's expecting to email me a Letter of Intent by the end of day Thursday. Why don't we plan to meet first thing on Friday morning?"

****

It was 6:30 a.m. and Alex had been lying awake for more than an hour. He got up and proceeded to the Starbucks down the street from his house and ordered the usual. He had to kill an hour and a half before his meeting with Peggy was scheduled to start.

He drove wide circles around the offices of EMC Capital Partners and parked at 7:45 a.m. Peggy greeted him in the hallway. They were the first to arrive at EMC that morning so Peggy turned on the office lights. Her body language gave away nothing of what was in the offer, despite having read it the night before.

Alex tried to look casual.

"I received a Letter of Intent from Print Technology Group last night."

"And . . .?"

Alex could wait no longer.

"I think you're going to like the offer," Peggy said as she handed it to Alex.

Alex took the document and started to read. His eyes quickly found the number. Print Technology Group was offering Alex $6 million for The Stapleton Agency. He wanted to display a calm façade for Peggy but he could feel his face turn red with excitement. He had worked so hard to transform The Stapleton Agency and finally someone was validating his work. This little business that Alex had started from a basement office in his home 10 years earlier was now worth $6 million!

Sensing that Alex needed to digest the offer, Peggy remained quiet for another minute.

"Alex, their offer is $6 million up front plus, if you achieve the revenue and profit projections in your three-year business plan, they'll pay you another $3 million in the form of an earn out. The offer is contingent on Print Technology Group completing a 60-day due diligence. They've asked us to give them exclusivity while they do their homework, which is pretty standard when big companies buy businesses of your size. If we want to accept the Letter of Intent, then we need to sign it back by September 15."

Alex left Peggy's office and called his wife to tell her the good news.

****

Alex sat silently as Ted read all six pages of the Print Technology Group Letter of Intent, making notes in the margin as he went. He turned to Alex.

"Congratulations, Alex. This is a big step for you. How do you feel?"

"I'm excited. It seems like such a long journey and we're almost there."

"Alex, this is a great offer but we're a long way from being finished. This is a non-binding Letter of Intent. They've asked for a two-month exclusivity period while they do their due diligence and a lot can happen over the next 60 days."

Alex had fixated on the number and had not read the entire document in detail. He was somewhat disappointed that Ted wasn't sharing in his excitement.

"Ted, this *is* a great offer and Print Technology Group is a great strategic fit for us. What concerns you about the offer?"

"This is a non-binding Letter of Intent. It's not the same thing as a binding offer. They can walk away from their offer at any time for any reason."

Alex looked deflated and Ted tried to cheer him up.

"Don't get me wrong, Alex. This is a great milestone for you and I think the Print Technology Group offer of six times your pre-tax profit this year is fair. I just don't want you to take the money to the bank yet."

Alex left Ted's office somewhat discouraged, realizing he was still a long way from selling his company.

Interrogation

Marcus instructed his associate David Reynolds to leave no stone unturned when investigating The Stapleton Agency.

David arrived at Alex's office early Monday morning. He adjusted his tortoiseshell glasses, and swung a large briefcase over his shoulder to release a hand, which he extended to introduce himself. Alex sequestered David in his office so as not to arouse suspicion among employees.

After some light banter, David began his interrogation.

"Alex, you claim there are 58,000 businesses in your immediate addressable market. Could you help me understand how you arrived at that number?"

Alex detailed all of the assumptions he and Ted had made in the calculation of the target market.

David was not satisfied. "I understand your math, Alex, but what I don't understand is why all of those companies would need a new logo. Isn't a logo something a company creates once?"

"A company logo is something businesses keep for a long time. That's why most of our business comes from creating product logos or new logos for spinoff divisions from companies we've worked with in the past."

"Yes, but surely companies don't create logos for each new product they launch."

"In our experience, companies create new logos for major product lines. For example, take Natural Foods. They are in the organic food business. When they decided to go into the ice cream business, they hired us to create the Natural Treats logo. They're now talking about launching a line of pet food and could need a new logo for that product line too."

"I'm sure Natural Foods is the exception," David said skeptically.

"Not really. Spring Valley Homes likes to create a new logo for each of their new development projects. We've been hired to produce three logos for Spring Valley in the last two years."

Finally, David seemed satisfied with the market size and moved on to probe Alex's process for hiring salespeople and his plans for expanding office space. David asked to see Alex's lease and a copy of every customer file. He pored over bank statements. He asked to read the Five-Step Logo Design Process instruction manual. The man had an insatiable appetite for information!

The grilling ended some time past 5:00 p.m. Alex needed a strong drink.

****

The next 45 days were among the most grueling of Alex's career. David's visit seemed to have increased his curiosity about the inner workings of The Stapleton Agency. Each line of questioning pulled a thread, which unfurled another long line of inquiries. Alex was glad to be meeting with Ted if for no other reason than to take a break from David's incessant interrogation.

"I'm starting to lose patience with Print Technology Group," Alex said.

"I thought you liked their business development guy. What was his name, Marcus something or other?"

"Yes, Marcus Knightsbridge is alright but he assigned a pit bull named David Reynolds to lead the due diligence process and he just can't seem to get enough information. Every document I send him triggers a request for three more."

"Due diligence is tough. David's job is to make sure Print Technology Group doesn't buy a dud. He will keep asking questions until Marcus calls him off. It sounds like you need to apply some pressure on Marcus."

"What do you propose?" Alex asked, intrigued by Ted's suggestion.

"They've had almost two months to investigate your business and you need to force them into a decision. It's time for a little strategic table pounding."

"Are you proposing I pitch some sort of fit?"

"Not necessarily a fit, but every negotiation reaches a point where you need to communicate to the other side that they've pushed you as far as they can. David's job is to ask questions so Marcus needs to hear directly from you that he's in jeopardy of losing this deal."

"What makes you so sure that Marcus will care if he loses the deal?"

"Marcus would have gone to his boss for approval to make the offer to buy you. They've just spent almost two months and hundreds of hours investigating your company and they're now invested in this deal. Marcus' job is to do deals and he is going to look silly if he wasted Print Technology Group's time with a deal that's not going ahead."

****

The phone call started off cordially enough with Marcus giving a summary of where they were at.

"David is keeping me in the loop with his work and we continue to be excited about the opportunity to bring The Stapleton Agency into the Print Technology Group family of companies."

"Thanks, Marcus. We're excited about the synergies as well, but I'm starting to get the sense you don't really want to do this deal. David has been hounding us for document after document. You've had almost two months to investigate us. If you can't make a decision based on the information you have to date, we're going to have to move on."

"Alex, I apologize if the process has been difficult. I'm sorry if we've given you the impression, at any point, that we're not interested in closing this deal. I'll check in with David and find out if there is anything else we need, but I'm fairly confident we're just about there."

"Can we agree to a closing date in the next two weeks?"

"I think that's possible. Let me check with my team and get back to you and Peggy via email."

14

The Finish Line

The meeting with Print Technology Group was scheduled for Monday, November 16 at the EMG Capital Partners office. Marcus agreed to a closing date of November 30 and wanted to discuss the results of their due diligence process with Alex and Peggy in person. He got straight to business.

"Alex, we continue to be excited about The Stapleton Agency."

Alex's heart sank as the tone of Marcus' voice revealed a 'but' was about to pass his lips.

"But the due diligence process has revealed some things that we're not entirely comfortable with."

After eight weeks of due diligence and six months of work with Peggy, Print Technology Group was about to yank the deal. Peggy sensed Alex's disappointment.

Peggy asked, "What exactly are you concerned about?"

"My colleague David was not entirely comfortable with the methodology used to size the market."

Instead of engaging in a debate, Peggy asked Marcus to lay his cards on the table.

"So what exactly are you saying?"

"We'd still very much like to do this deal but the valuation model we used to arrive at the original offer in our Letter of Intent doesn't hold up based on the new information we gleaned from the due diligence process. As a result, we're adjusting our offer to $5,200,000 up front. We're leaving the earn out piece untouched."

Alex couldn't believe his ears. He thought they had a deal in principle. He knew himself well enough to know that he needed to leave the room before he said something he would regret.

Sensing that Alex was upset, Peggy quickly adjourned the meeting with a promise to get back to Marcus by the end of the week.

****

Alex spent most of Monday afternoon stalking around his office. He didn't sleep well on Monday evening so by the time he arrived at Ted's office, his nerves were frayed. He found it cathartic to rant to Ted.

"I can't believe they want to change the deal two weeks before we're supposed to close. We had a deal. I agreed to move forward based on an up-front valuation of $6 million and they're lopping almost 20 percent off the price because some weasel in a back office didn't like one of my spreadsheets."

Ted let him blow off steam. Finally, sensing Alex had calmed down, Ted weighed in.

"Alex, I wish I could tell you I was surprised, but I'm not."

"You knew this was going to happen?" Alex asked, directing his frustration towards Ted for the first time.

"It's very common for a company to lower their offer price after the due diligence process. They know they have you cornered and your only two choices are to accept the lower price or walk. Of the four businesses I sold, three of them closed with a lower price than was originally proposed in the Letter of Intent."

"I'm going to tell them to go to hell!" Alex exclaimed, still steaming about what he saw as Print Technology Group's dishonorable negotiation tactic.

"Alex, that's your right and I would understand if you chose to walk away. But before you do that, I want you to go back to your office and find the envelope I had you put in a safe place. Open it up and study it before you call Peggy."

The Envelope

Back at his office, Alex unlocked his desk drawer and saw the sealed envelope he had left there almost a year ago. He opened the letter and pulled out the single recipe card inside. There, written in his own handwriting, Alex saw the number he had dreamed of selling The Stapleton Agency for more than a year ago: *$5,000,000*

He held the card in his hand as he gazed down at the number. He thought about all of his work over the past few years. He remembered John Stevens and how dependent they once were on First National Bank. He thought about Elijah Kaplan, Tony Martino, and the rest of the mediocre team he had settled for to create second-rate advertising campaigns. He thought about how good Chris and his team had become at creating logos. He thought about the late night calls to Mary Pradham and why he wanted to sell his business in the first place, and how he went about calculating his dream check.

He smiled for the first time in 48 hours and called Peggy to give her the news.

"I'm prepared to accept the lower offer provided Print Technology Group closes on November 30. If they stall or delay at all, I'm out."

"I think you've made a good decision, Alex. I'll call Marcus."

"Just make sure we get this done by the 30th."

The Closing

The morning of November 30 was spent at Print Technology Group's law firm. Alex's signature was required on a variety of documents. After he was finished and the obligatory congratulations were offered, Alex excused himself. He got in his Range Rover and drove with no particular destination in mind. The trees whisked by as he reached cruising speed. Suddenly he felt the vibration of his mobile receiving an email; it was a message from Mary Pradham at First National Bank.

> *Alex: We've just received a rather large wire transfer into your personal account from Print Technology Group. Please call me when you get a chance as I'd like to give you some suggestions for investing these funds.*

Alex smiled and kept driving.

The Model for Selling Your Business

Like Alex Stapleton, many business owners find themselves trapped in an unsellable business. Clients ask to deal with the owner, the owner becomes personally involved in delivering the project, reinforcing the client's reliance on the owner, and the cycle continues. A business reliant on its owner is unsellable so the owner becomes trapped in the business.

To transform a service firm into a sellable company, follow this 8-step process. Before you start the process, engage a good accountant with experience in helping entrepreneurs with succession planning. Depending on your tax jurisdiction, there will be tax planning strategies your accountant can put into place now that will minimize your tax bill when you sell your business. *Do not wait until you have an offer to see an accountant.* Timing is critical; get an accountant to devise a tax minimization strategy *before* you start the 8 steps.

Step 1: Create a Standard Service Offering
The first step in building a sellable company is to find a service your clients find valuable that you can teach someone else to perform. Brainstorm all of the services that you provide today

and plot them on a simple diagram with "Teachable" on one axis and "Client Value" on the other.

Often, you'll find the most teachable services are the ones that clients value the least. That's normal. Alternatively, you'll probably find the services your clients value most are the least teachable. Work through all of the services you offer and eliminate services that a client needs to buy only once. Of the remaining services, pick the one that is plotted closest to the top right corner of the diagram above, which means that clients both value it as a service *and* you can teach it to someone to execute. This becomes the Standard Service Offering.

Sometimes you'll find that, by combining one or more services, you can create the ideal offering. Experiment with bundling a few services together to stake out the top right corner of the diagram.

Once you've isolated the service that clients value, need often, and is teachable, document your process for executing this type of project. You'll recall the conversation when Ted helped Alex to define and document the Five-Step Logo Design Process. Define each of the steps so that you can repeat the model in the same way each time.

Once you have a Standard Service Offering, write an instruction manual to deliver it. Make sure your instructions are specific enough for someone to follow independently by using examples and fill-in-the-blank templates where possible. Test your instructions by asking someone or a team to deliver the service without your involvement.

Getting the instruction manual done right will take time. Expect it to go through many drafts. Be patient.

Next, name your Standard Service Offering. Naming your offering gives you ownership of it and help you differentiate from potential competitors. Once you are the owner of something unique, you move from offering a commoditized service to one where you decide the terms of its use. There's a market for whatever generic service you provide and you don't want customers comparing your price to others. Instead, name your offering and each of the steps you take to deliver it to differentiate the service so that you can set the price and payment terms.

Once you've named your Standard Service offering and each of the steps, write a short description of the features and corresponding benefits of each step. Once you have the steps to your process and the corresponding description copy, revamp all of your customer communications (e.g., website, brochure) to describe your process.

Step 2: Create a Positive Cash Flow Cycle
Next, create a positive cash flow cycle by charging up front for your Standard Service Offering. This will be possible if you

141

branded your offering properly. Depending on your service, you may not be able to charge for the entire amount in advance, but you can try. You'll be surprised at how many clients agree. It's not unheard of to have clients pay $100,000 or more up front for a Standard Service Offering that is delivered over a year. If you charge up front, you will create a positive cash flow cycle, which will give you the cash you need to operate without diluting yourself with other shareholders. Acquiring companies will also give you a higher valuation when you sell your company because they will not have to commit as much of their own capital to your company.

Step 3: Hire a Sales Team

Once you have created, packaged, and started to charge for a Standard Service Offering, you need to remove yourself from selling it. If you have others delivering the service, but you're still the rainmaker, you will not be able to sell your businesses without a long and risky earn out. Instead, you need to hire salespeople. If you have done a good job packaging a consistent service, the best salespeople will be those used to selling a product. Look for salespeople like Angie Thacker who enjoy selling first and the product second. Avoid salespeople who come from professional services companies, as they will want to re-invent your service for every client.

If at all possible, hire at least two salespeople (not just one). Salespeople are competitive and an acquirer will want to see that you have a product that can be sold by salespeople in general and not just one superstar salesperson.

Step 4: Stop Accepting Other Projects

The next step is to stop taking on projects that fall outside of your Standard Service Offering. It's tempting to accept these projects because they bolster your revenue and cash flow. If you're charging up front for your service and your salespeople are selling it, then you shouldn't have to worry about cash flow. That leaves revenue as the reason to accept these projects that fall outside of your process. The revenue may feel good at first but it comes at an unacceptable cost: your team will lose focus; realizing that you're not serious about your process, clients will see a chink in your armor and start asking for customization of their projects; and you will need to hire other people to deliver. Most importantly, when you go to present your business to an acquirer, they will see the mixture of revenue from both your Standard Service Offering and project work and determine that you're just another service business.

I've had the opportunity to speak with hundreds of business owners who have made this transition and most have told me that clients who used to ask for custom services respect the change they made to their business model. Many clients actually buy more once the service is standardized. Clients are smart; they often know you're overreaching your capabilities in accepting assignments that fall outside of your sweet spot. In most cases, they will use you for these services because they know, like, and trust you. That doesn't mean you need to accept them.

Stopping yourself from accepting projects outside of your Standard Service Offering is the toughest part of the process of creating a sellable company. You will have employees testing your resolve and clients asking for exceptions, and you will second-guess yourself on more than one occasion. This is normal; you have to be strong on this and resist the temptation.

There is a point where the wind will start blowing the other way and your clients, employees, and stakeholders will finally realize that you're serious about focusing on one thing. It takes time. It will happen, and when it does and you feel like the boat has actually shifted, you will have taken a giant step in creating a sellable company.

Once you have focused on a Standard Service Offering for which you charge up front, and you have sales reps who are capable of selling and employees who are capable of delivering without your involvement, you need to create a two-year run of increasing business and financial performance. This is often frustrating for business owners who have made the decision to sell their business. Be patient and remember that these two years will dramatically increase the cash you get up front for your business and minimize your reliance on an earn out.

Expect the year that you make the switch from accepting projects to focusing on your Standard Service Offering to be a bad financial year on paper. Your cash flow should be fine if you're charging up front but your accountant will need to change the way he or she recognizes revenue by spreading it out over the life of the delivery period of your Standard Service Offering. This has the effect of lowering your revenue in the current period and allowing you to go into future months with revenue on the books.

Spend the two years driving the model as far and fast as you can. Avoid the temptation to get personally involved in selling or delivering your Standard Service Offering. Instead, when you get asked for help, diagnose the problem and fix your system so the problem doesn't recur.

Many business owners realize a tremendous uptick in their quality of life in these two years. Business improves, cash flow grows, and client headaches decrease. In fact, many business owners like this stage so much, they shelve their plans to sell their company and decide to run it in perpetuity. If this happens to you, congratulations! If you still want to sell your business, continue on to the next step.

Step 5: Launch a Long-Term Incentive Plan for Managers

You need to prove to a buyer that you have a management team who can run the business after you're gone. What's more, you need to show that the management team is locked into staying with your company after acquisition.

Avoid using equity to retain key management as it will unnecessarily complicate the sale process. Instead, create a long-term incentive plan for your key managers. Each year, take an amount equivalent to their annual bonus and put it aside in a long-term incentive account earmarked for each manager you want to retain. Allow the manager to withdraw one third of the pool each year after a three-year period. That way, a good manager must always walk away from a significant amount of money should they decide to leave your company. You can go to www.BuiltToSell.com to find a template for a long-term incentive plan.

Step 6: Find a Broker

For those business owners who are committed to selling, the next step in the process is to find representation. If your company has less than $2 million in sales, a business broker will best serve you. If you have more than $2 million in sales, a boutique mergers & acquisitions firm is probably your best bet. Look for a firm with experience in your industry, as they already know many of the potential buyers for your business. To find an M&A firm or business broker, ask other entrepreneurs you know who have sold their firm for a recommendation.

Make sure your broker appreciates what you have done to transform your business. If they continue to see you as the same as the commoditized service providers in your industry, move on. They need to appreciate that you have created something special and deserve to be compensated at a higher rate.

Once you have an M&A firm or broker engaged, they'll work with you to create The Book. This document describes your business and its performance to date along with a business plan for the future.

Your broker will typically charge a percentage of the proceeds of the deal in the form of a success fee.

Step 7: Tell Your Management Team

Your broker will set up management presentations for you and your team to meet with a prospective buyer. Telling your management team can be a daunting task. Think about it from their perspective and make sure there is something in it for them if the deal goes through. An acquisition can often mean significant career opportunities for your managers and that may be enough. Emphasize that, by being acquired, your managers will be more likely to hit the personal bonus targets, which will benefit them twice if you have created a long-term incentive plan as described in Step 5. You may also want to offer key employees a simple success bonus if a deal goes through.

Offer to pay the success bonus in two installments, with one installment coming 60 days after the close and the other at some point in the future. An acquirer will like the fact that you put a deal-related incentive in place for your key employees to stay.

Step 8: Convert Offer(s) to a Binding Deal
Once you have completed your management presentations, you will hopefully get some offers in the form of a non-binding Letter of Intent. As you review it, keep in mind that your advisor will be trying to sell the benefits of the offer to you because:

a) they'll get paid if the deal goes through; and
b) they want to remind you of the hard work they have done to justify their fee.

This is normal and to be expected, but do not be swayed by it. Study the offer. It will likely contain an amount of money (or some other currency like stock) up front with another chunk tied to one or more performance targets for your business after the sale, which is often referred to as an earn out.

Treat the earn out portion as gravy. *An earn out is simply a way for an acquirer to minimize their risk in buying your company.* This means that you take most of the risk and they get most of the reward. Some earn outs have proven lucrative for the owners who accepted them. Most business owners who have sold a service business, however, have a nightmare story to share involving an overbearing parent company not delivering on what they promised in an earn out contract. As long as you get what you want for the business up front, and treat the earn out as gravy, you can walk when things get nasty. If you feel like you have to stay to get full value for the business, then life will get uncomfortable for the duration of the earn out.

Keep in mind that the Letter of Intent is usually not a binding offer. Unless it includes a break-up fee (rare for smaller companies), they have every right to walk and you get nothing. Deals often fall through in the due diligence period, so don't be surprised if it happens to you.

The due diligence period usually lasts 60 – 90 days and a veteran entrepreneur I know likes to refer to it as the entrepreneur's "proctology exam." It isn't fun and the best strategy is often to just survive it. Due diligence can make you feel vulnerable and exposed. If the buyer is a professional, they will dispatch a team of MBA-types to your office who will quickly identify the weak spots in your model. That's their job. Try to keep your cool during this period. Try to present things in the best possible light but do not lie or hide the facts.

Once the due diligence period is over, there is a good chance that the offer in the Letter of Intent will be discounted. Again, don't be surprised if this happens to you. Expect it and you'll be pleasantly surprised if it doesn't happen. You'll need to go back to the math you did when reviewing the Letter in the first place. If the new discounted offer meets your target cash up front, then you can go ahead and agree. If the discounted offer falls below the threshold, walk away no matter how much the acquirer promises to help you hit your earn out.

If you accept the revised offer or the due diligence period ends, you'll have a closing meeting. Typically held at the acquirer's law firm, this is where the formalities are handled. You sign a lot of documents and, once the documents are signed, the law firm will move the cash portion of the sale from their account to yours. The deal is done.

Are you curious to see if you have built a sellable business? Do you want to know how much someone might pay to buy your business? Visit www.BuiltToSell.com and take the Sellability Index quiz.

Recommended Reading & Resources

Join *The Strategic Coach*
The folks at The Strategic Coach are the gurus on building a company and a life. They created the concept of a Standard Service Offering, which they call a Unique Process. They will help you articulate and implement your process. www.strategiccoach.com

Read *The E-Myth* and get an E-Myth Coach
Michael Gerber coined the term "working *on* the business not *in* the business" in his best-seller *The E-Myth Revisited*. But don't just read the book; get yourself into one of the E-Myth coaching programs. www.e-myth.com

Follow Tim Ferris
Timothy Ferris wrote *The 4-Hour Work Week* and will have you spinning on what to do with your time after you have sold your company. www.fourhourworkweek.com

Attend any event produced by Verne Harnish
Verne Harnish runs Gazelles and is the author of *Mastering the Rockefeller Habits*. He's a growth guru and his company specializes in educating and coaching growth companies. Make sure to sign up for his must-read Weekly Insights. www.gazelles.com

Read *Small Giants*
Bo Burlingham has chronicled the entrepreneurial life for years in the pages of *Inc.* magazine. *Small Giants* will inspire you to focus on being great at doing one thing instead of spreading yourself too thin by grasping for "bad revenue." www.smallgiantsbook.com

Read everything Norm Brodsky has ever written
Norm is a legend among entrepreneurs. He has started seven businesses and writes a column for *Inc.* magazine (back issues at www.inc.com).

Subscribe to Small Business Trends
Anita Campbell is a multimedia maven of small business insight. She tweets, blogs, and writes to hundreds of thousands of small business owners each month. www.smallbiztrends.com

Read *Duct Tape Marketing*
John Jantsch will give you practical advice on how to market your business. His book is a crisp read and his site is a must. www.ducttapemarketing.com

Read *Topgrading* and *Topgrading for Sales*
You'll learn about a great formula for hiring people, including the salespeople you'll need to drive your sales engine without you. www.smarttopgrading.com

Read *Brand: It Ain't the logo*
Learn how to create a brand that is independent from you.

More resources and advice for creating a sellable business are available at www.BuiltToSell.com

Acknowledgements

They say that it takes a village to raise a child. I feel the same way about writing a book. This project is the sum total of what I have learned in business from starting and ultimately exiting four businesses. My first business was a flop and I probably would have stopped there had it not been for the help, encouragement, and guidance of an incredible set of mentors. Ted Matthews combines Seth Godin's marketing savvy with Mother Teresa's heart. Thank you, Ted. Other teachers include Michael de Pencier, David Drew, Jay Gordon, Bruce MacLellan, Louise Mitchell, Rob Paterson, Dan Sullivan, and Dan Taylor.

Bo Burlingham is one of many authors who gave their time and talent. Other authors who helped with inspiration and advice include Jim Blasigame, Anita Campbell, Tom Deans, John Ellett, Verne Harnish, John Brown, Shep Hyken, John Jantsch, and Rich Sloan.

Andrea Nickel and Perry Miele at Beringer Capital taught me about the mysterious world of mergers and acquisitions. Beringer is a boutique firm that punches well above its weight. Other smart people I leaned on for advice on the mechanics of doing a deal include Randy Cochran, Ron Dersch, Ritch and Mike Epstein, Michael Henry, Diane Neiderman, Steve Parrish, George Rossolatos, Rob Slee, and Colin Walker.

A handful of small business market thought leaders encouraged this project, including Doug Case at Wells Fargo, Elisa Cool and Evan Blank at *The Wall Street Journal*, Steve Chadwick at Verizon Wireless, Kareem Chouli at VISA, Barry Ellison at BDC, Glauco Ferrari and Cindy Bates at Microsoft, Walter Good and Wendy Vinson at The E-Myth Worldwide, Mike Handelsman at BizBuySell.com, Deborah Herman at SunTrust, Beth Horowitz at Discover Network, Noel Hulsman and Teena Poirier at *The Globe & Mail*, Bob Lapointe at *Inc.* magazine, Shane Lawrence at TD, Randy McCollum at Administaff, Kyle McNamara and Dave Wilton at Scotiabank, Jeff Parker at US Bank, Bruno Perreault at MasterCard, Derrick Ragland and Stephen Miller at HSBC, Karen Ripperger at The Principal, Karen Sawyer and James Wong at BMO, Karen Larrimer at PNC, Susan Sobbott, Howard Grosfield, and Denise Pickett at American Express, and Keith Williams and Becky Roemen at Entrepreneurs' Organization (EO).

My EO forum mates Mike Boydell, Sam Ifergan, Steve Horst, Sean Hunt, Joe Stutzman, and Dean Tai shared a lifetime of business and personal experiences with me.

Thank you to Penny Sansevieri, along with Sandy Diaz and her team at Smith, for getting the word out. Cameron Drew helped me to navigate the wacky world of book distribution. Thank you to Ross, Rod, and Jennifer at Highspot for managing the book publishing process and to my friends at Loft Communications who gave me a place to write.

I tortured many friends by forcing them to read early drafts and concepts for this book. To Rich Cooper, Liane Hunt, Simon Tuplin, and Trevor Currie, thank you for seeing through the typos and making this a better book.

Thanks to my sister Emma (she's the smart one), who taught me that there is a difference between wanting to sell a business and wanting to create a sellable business.

Mom, thanks for encouraging me to read and write even though I couldn't stand doing either when I was young. Thanks for teaching me to count to ten backward before a big speech and for being the very first copy editor of this book. Dad, you taught me everything I know about business and being a father and I'll always try to be half as good as you were at both.

To JB and The Lads, you make it all worthwhile.

John Warrillow is an entrepreneur, author, and speaker. Throughout his career, John has started and exited four companies. Most recently he transformed Warrillow & Co. from a boutique consultancy—specializing in studying and reporting on the small business market—into a recurring revenue model subscription business, which he sold in 2008 to The Corporate Executive Board (NASDAQ: EXBD). He is the author of *Drilling for Gold: How Corporations Can Successfully Market to Small Businesses* (Wiley: New York, 2002) and founding producer of the nationally syndicated radio feature Today's Entrepreneur. In 2008, John was recognized by *BtoB* magazine's "Who's Who" list as one of America's most influential business-to-business marketers.

Do you know a business owner who needs to read Built To Sell?
Order more copies using the form below.

Fax to 647-439-0871 or visit www.BuiltToSell.com

Name: _____

Address: _____

City: _____   State/Province: _____

Zip/Postal Code: _____   Phone: _____

Email: _____

Ship to (if different from above):

Name: _____

Address: _____

City: _____   State/Province: _____

Zip/Postal Code: _____   Phone: _____

Quantity	Price per Copy*
1	$17.95 USD
2–5	$15.95 USD
6–9	$14.95 USD
10–49	$12.95 USD
50+	$9.95 USD

Quantity Ordered = [   ]

* Plus applicable taxes and shipping. Price listed is for softcover edition. Books ship the same day that orders are received and typically arrive within 4 or 5 business days. For additional shipping options, please order from www.BuiltToSell.com

Credit Card Type : ☐ VISA   ☐ MasterCard   ☐ American Express

Credit Card #: _____

Exp. Date: _____   CCV Code: _____

Name on Card: _____

Signature for Credit Card: _____